THE HOUR OF INSIGHT:

A SEQUEL TO

Moments of Personal Discovery

THE HOUR OF INSIGHT:

A SEQUEL TO

Moments of Personal Discovery

EDITED BY

Robert M. MacIver

Essay Index Reprint Series

Originally published by
THE INSTITUTE for RELIGIOUS and SOCIAL STUDIES

 BOOKS FOR LIBRARIES PRESS
FREEPORT, NEW YORK

Originally published as part of
Religion and Civilization Series.

Copyright, 1954 by
The Institute for Religious and Social Studies.

Reprinted 1972 by arrangement with
Harper & Row Publishers, Inc.

Library of Congress Cataloging in Publication Data

Institute for Religious and Social Studies,
    Jewish Theological Seminary of America.
    The hour of insight.

    (Essay index reprint series)
    Original ed. issued in series: Religion and
civilization series.
    "Based on lectures given at The Institute for
Religious and Social Studies of The Jewish Theological
Seminary of America during the winter of 1952-1953."
    1. Inspiration. 2. Civilization--Addresses,
essays, lectures. I. MacIver, Robert Morrison,
1852-1970, ed. II. Title. III. Series: Religion
and civilization series.
[BF410.I5 1972]   153.2'5   70-167366
ISBN 0-8369-2655-2

PRINTED IN THE UNITED STATES OF AMERICA
BY
NEW WORLD BOOK MANUFACTURING CO., INC.
HALLANDALE, FLORIDA 33009

This volume is based on lectures given at The Institute for Religious and Social Studies of The Jewish Theological Seminary of America during the winter of 1952–1953. Unfortunately, Doctor Andrew W. Cordier could not write for publication his address in the series. Each chapter in this volume represents solely the individual opinion of the author.

CONTENTS

PREFACE

The reception of the first series of "Moments of Discovery" was so cordial that a second series was arranged for the Institute luncheon meetings held during the winter of 1952–1953. Readers who welcomed the first series will find the second no less revealing and even more diversified than the earlier one. Two scientists, both exploring the unfathomed complex of interdependence between what we unknowingly call mind and body, tell of the insights they have gained. A historian of science reflects on the processes of discovery in the light of his own experience. An anthropologist who does not disdain to call herself also a "housewife" makes that very fact the first step in the understanding of the simpler peoples, not without a moral for the "civilized." An artist relates how his own life-experience led him on the quest for the intrinsic form beneath the show of things. A judge describes the vicissitudes and conjunctures which impelled him to become a crusader for genuine justice. An historian of American letters finds that something seems to stall the maturation of American authors. A writer widely known for his brilliant "detective stories" discovers the necessity for world government. A professor of English literature relates how he turned belatedly to religion to find "newness of life." A distinguished Jewish authority tells how he attained a serenity of outlook that stems back to his first recognition, in the circle of the family, of disinterested love, and how this has sustained him in a world still torn by hatreds. And a professor of religion beautifully tells the story of the first intimation that came to her concerning the nature of the mystery of religion.

The diversity of the contents is a sample of the diversity of the ways in which men experience significance in a world that opens up so many aspects to so many seeking minds. It is for each to find his own and therewith to respect and perchance learn from the reports of others who have sincerely sought a light to guide their paths.

THE EDITOR

THE HOUR OF INSIGHT:

A SEQUEL TO

Moments of Personal Discovery

I

THE A-HA! PHENOMENON

BY

HUDSON HOAGLAND

Certain psychologists have referred to the "a-ha phenomenon." Each professional scientist cherishes the all too rare occasions when a flash of insight surging up from his unconscious leads him to say, "A-ha, that's it!" and then drives him on to crack a technical problem that had hitherto defeated him. The frequency with which the a-ha phenomenon occurs to an investigator is a measure of the satisfaction that he derives from his work. I would like to give a few personal examples to illustrate this experience.

After taking my bachelor's degree at Columbia in 1921, I spent three years at the Massachusetts Institute of Technology in training to become a chemical engineer. It had always been understood that I would enter my family's manufacturing business in New Jersey and the engineering training was an automatic consequence of this expectancy. I had been married during my last undergraduate year to the daughter of Wendell Bush, Professor of Philosophy at Columbia, and through him I had been fortunate in coming to know Professor Dewey, Professor Woodridge, and other members of the Philosophy Department whom I greatly respected. As a result of these contacts and my undergraduate courses I had become excited about aspects of philosophy which led me to interests remote from the field of engineering in which I was specializing. In 1924, my graduate work had taken me to the Lackawanna Steel Plant in Buffalo for field experience where I became engaged in an investigation of the design of nozzles for the burning of coal tar in open hearth furnaces. One evening, after an especially frustrating day studying how fast tar could flow through pipes, I wandered into the Buffalo Free Public Library and picked from the shelf a journal containing an article by Professor L. T. Troland of the Psychology Department of Harvard University. This was a rather popular description and review of the conduction of the nerve impulse, and to my astonishment I learned for the first time that one could measure the passage of electrical nerve messages in animals by applying electrodes to the nerves and connecting them to suitable recording apparatus. Here it seemed to me was a remarkable physical approach to the mysteries of behavior and conduct. Electrophysiology seemed to combine a procedure for investigating the age old mind-body problem with the physical technics that I had learned in my engineering studies. I was, of course, a very naive youngster, but this paper, more than perhaps anything I had ever read, produced a flash of the a-ha phenomenon that quite literally changed my life. Apparently I had never wanted much to be an industrial engineer anyway, for a few weeks later I went to Harvard to interview Professor Troland with the idea of becoming his graduate student as soon as I received my engineering degree in June.

Circumstances prevented my actually working with Professor Troland, but I registered at Harvard as a graduate student in psychology in the fall of 1924 and ultimately took my Ph.D. in 1927, doing most of my work, including my thesis, in physiology under the direction of Professor W. J. Crozier. My subsequent professional appointments and work have been in the field of physiology and biochemistry. It is indeed interesting to see how the reading of one article at a critical time, against a particular background of interests, triggered the revision of my professional life.

I should like now to give another example of the a-ha phenomenon as it developed in relation to a specific research problem. It is clear to anyone who stops to think about it that rhythms of behavior cycles are commonplace. Our breathing movements are rhythmical; our heartbeat is rhythmical; sex cycles of animals, such as the menstrual periods, are rhythmical, as are peristaltic movements in the digestive tract. The nerve message, which can be thought of as a sort of basic unit of behavior is an electrochemical change that sweeps rapidly over the nerve fiber. Billions of these fibers course about in the brain and spinal cord and connect the brain centers to sense organs which furnish information about our environment. Other nerve fibers run from the brain to the muscles to make us respond to events about us with, we hope, appropriate behavior. One impulse follows another in rhythmical fashion and travels along the nerve as a discrete pulse or wave of electrochemical change which can be studied in detail in the living tissue by modern electronic and photographic equipment. The frequency or number of nerve impulses per unit time passing over nerve fibers to the central nervous system informs us of the intensity of sensory experience. In like manner, the strength of contraction of our muscles is determined by the frequency of nerve impulses passing over the motor nerve fibers to them from the central nervous system. All behavior, be it the reflex response to a pin prick, or the composition of a great work of art, depends upon the patterned integration of nerve impulses in the central nervous system. The brain itself is continually active, producing integrated electrical waves of characteristic patterns from millions of cells rhythmically discharging in groups. The frequencies and patterns of these waves, which can be recorded by suitable apparatus, are modified by various states of consciousness and levels of activity and are important signs of brain function. The chemical basis underlying these rhythmic events in the nervous system has been a matter of great interest to me for many years.

Everyone who has had a course in elementary chemistry knows that heat makes chemical change go faster. A well known mathematical equation, the Arrhenius equation, describes the relation between temperature and the speed of simple chemical processes. It has been shown that even complicated chemical processes in living cells usually obey this equation. A constant in the equation may characterize the nature of a specific controlling chemical reaction that regulates a whole sequence of chemical processes involved, for example, in the release of usable energy from the burning of a foodstuff like sugar in living cells. Substances called enzymes in the cells regulate in stepwise fashion the destruction of the energy yielding molecules of foodstuffs. If we consider for a moment the analogy of a group of men at an assembly bench taking apart an airplane motor, it may help us to picture how a group of enzymes dismantles a sugar molecule. At the bench we find that the operation of one man will inevitably be slower than that of the others. This is because of differences in the difficulty of operative procedures from man to man and differences in the individuals' effectiveness. The number of airplane motors which thus get disassembled in a day will depend upon the speed of operation of the slowest man at the bench who is a bottleneck, or pacemaker, for the process. In like manner, foodstuff molecules are taken apart or metabolized by organic catalysts or enzymes acting in sequential steps in the cell. The slowest link in this chain of chemical reactions may serve as the pacemaker for the release of energy to be utilized by the tissues. A constant in the Arrhenius equation, called the activation energy, may designate the chemical nature of this slowest step. We find that a limited number of these slow steps, corresponding to a dozen or so enzyme systems common to most animal cells, regulate the energy metabolism of a wide variety of cellular systems. This indicates that from one organized cell system to another, now one and now another enzyme system is the limiting factor for the release of energy to do useful work.

During the 1920's, in the laboratory of Crozier at Harvard, we found that a great number of waves and rhythms of action of animals— breathing rhythms, heartbeat rhythms, rhythms of cilia beats and of insect movements—follow this equation as a function of temperature and the values of the activation energy turned out to be identical with those usually encountered in direct chemical studies of the oxygen consumption and carbon dioxide production of isolated cell systems. The implication of this is that the frequency of such a rhythm is directly proportional to the speed of some basic underlying chemical pacemaker system controlling oxidation or metabolism within the cells. During the 1930's I showed that certain electrical brain waves in men followed this equation when the men had their internal temperatures changed by giving them artificial fevers. I found that the activation energies for the frequencies of the brain waves were identical with those that we obtained from certain brain enzyme systems that we could isolate from the tissues which normally regulate the rate at which the brain cells use oxygen brought to them by the circulating blood.

One day in 1932 my wife fell ill with influenza and ran a temperature of 104°F. I was quite concerned about her. She asked me to do an errand at the drug store which took perhaps ten minutes but when I returned she insisted that I must have been gone for at least half an hour. This remark surprised me and after the usual husband-wife argument I experienced the "a-ha phenomenon." In a flash it came to me that her elevated body temperature was producing more rapid biochemical changes in her brain and that accordingly clock-time, which for public convenience we have standardized against the motions of the heavenly bodies, appeared to her to be abnormally prolonged. More chemical events were taking place in her fevered brain in a given interval of clock-time than would take place at normal body temperature, and as these events would be her standard for the judgment of time she would incorrectly think that much more physical time had passed than had actually done so. I immediately rushed to the laboratory for a stopwatch and a notebook and pencil and asked her to count for me at a speed she believed to be one per second up to sixty. She is a musician with a good sense of interval. I timed her speed of counting repeatedly for the next three days and took her temperature for each count while her temperature went from 104° to 97°F. She had no idea why I wanted her to count but was a very good sport about it all. I then applied the Arrhenius equation to her rhythm of counting as a function of her temperature and found a remarkably good fit of the equation to the counting data—in fact, as good a fit as might have been obtained in a chemical experiment in the laboratory. The activation energy, calculated from the equation which is indicative of the limiting chemical step regulating her counting, was identical with one that had been encountered on various occasions in studies of the rhythmic activities of coldblooded animals and in studies of the oxygen consumption of isolated cell systems studied under different temperatures in thermostats. The data indicated that the speed of a continuous chemical reaction going on somewhere, presumably in the brain, is the standard against which we judge time.

I next proceeded to study the time sense of normal volunteers by giving them artificial fever and found that the equation fitted the data and gave the same activation energy from person to person as characteristic of the human time sense. This seemed to me to be a very exciting discovery. Because clock-time depends on relative motion of the heavenly bodies, our subjective time sense depends on the relative motions of molecules in the regulation of the burning of foodstuffs.

It is rather appalling to think of the kind of world we might live in if we did not possess a beautifully precise apparatus for keeping our internal body temperature constant around 98°F. All animals, other than birds and mammals, lack this thermostat for regulating their internal temperatures. To such animals a continuous time scale flowing at a constant rate from past to future, such as we have adopted as our public standard of time, would be meaningless. For a difference of 50°F between summer and winter, time must pass for the so-called "coldblooded" animals—frogs, reptiles, insects—roughly ten times as fast in winter as it does in summer, for a chilled nervous system would slow time as a warmed one speeds it according to the Arrhenius equation. What kind of public time standard would we have devised if we lived in a world with a time warp of this order of magnitude? If an hour in a warm house corresponded to sixty subjective minutes, an hour out-of-doors on a winter's day would seem to us six minutes long! Public timekeeping without our physiological thermostats would indeed be a problem.

There are, of course, many other factors that modify our sense of time. These I have discussed elsewhere and shall not consider at the moment. All of these considerations, however, are consistent with the view of a private chemical clock in the brain such as I have outlined.

A startling corollary of the views we have been considering is the possibility of modifying an organism's private time scale so much that for all practical purpose it may be projected intact far into the future by making its particular time stand still. This would be analogous in a way to the theme of H. G. Wells' charming story, *The Time Machine*.

One day in talking with my children about the "time capsule" buried at the site of the New York World's Fair, to be opened 5,000 years hence, one of them remarked how exciting it would be if we could be present to see the public response to this event. That night, while drifting off to sleep, it occurred to me that if a man could be chilled throughout uniformly in one second to a temperature around the absolute zero of only minus 463°F he would not have time to freeze, because crystallization of his body water requires time. All his tissues might pass into a reversible vitreous state. If, after five thousand years at the low temperature, the man were warmed uniformly to his normal body temperature of 98°F in one second, he should resume his life where he had left it off with all memories intact and not a minute older than he was at the time of chilling, for aging is a matter of chemical deterioration. I knew that to send a man on such a time journey into the future is impossible because of the large heat capacity of water which comprises most of his body and the fact that we live at only about 560°F above this absolute zero (*i.e.*, 463 + 98). At the absolute zero of minus 463°F all molecular motion—all chemical and physical change—is stopped and time must stand still, as time is by its very nature a product of relative motion. This short temperature range from the absolute zero to that of our internal body temperature is only a few hundred degrees and could not furnish a strong heat-removing gradient so that the inner parts of large organisms could not be cooled rapidly and at the same rates as outer parts. In organisms of microscopic dimensions however this situation need not apply. A man could not be cooled uniformly at a rate of 500 degrees per second and would die by water crystal formation which would disrupt his tissue cells. Very small organisms that can be cooled and warmed very rapidly have, however, been projected into the future and an experimental literature existed on this subject.

As a result of this midnight thought, Gregory Pincus and I did some experiments and found that sixty per cent of human sperm cells could survive to full normal motility after dunking in liquid nitrogen at minus 320°F. We further found that the vitrified sperm could be stored in dry ice at minus 112°F and that the percentage of sperm that were motile on rapid warming to 98°F was not affected significantly by the length of time they were stored, whether for a matter of seconds or of months. Time has been practically stopped for these sperm cells.

While a man could not be projected into the future it is thus possible that his immediate offspring might be, provided the fertilizing powers as well as the motility of the sperm were unimpaired. Women might thus have offspring by men long since dead and sperm banks of heroes of the past could perhaps, in the dreary world of Orwell's *1984,* be used for artificial insemination. But this deplorable picture has little to do with the discussion today and is not one that I recommend to your serious consideration. Studies of this kind can have practical significance for animal husbandry were it possible to chill and store the viable sperm of distinguished race horses and valuable cattle for use generations later. Very recently A. S. Parkes in England has obtained calves from artificial insemination with chilled and stored sperm.

It is interesting to trace the ramification of ideas involved in the foregoing example of discovery. From a background interest in rhythms of activity of the nervous system and the chemical events that regulate them, my wife's fever and her reproach concerning the length of time taken by my drug store visit triggered experiments on the effect of temperature on the time sense. These experiments led to the view that subjective time is regulated by a chemical reaction system giving us our concept of the constant unidirectional flow of time. This view of time would not be possible without our thermostats that closely regulate internal body temperature at $98.4° \pm 2°F$. As sidereal time is measured by the motion of the heavenly bodies, so our private time is measured by the motions of specific molecules. If all motion stops, all time must stop—sidereal and personal. All motion does stop at the absolute zero of minus $463°F$. We found experimentally that we could stop and start again the time of individual small organisms by rapid temperature changes in accordance with expectations from physicochemical theory and as a consequence of this there emerged some potentially exciting implications in relation to mammalian sperm cells and heredity.

During the early years of my professional life I was fortunate in being interested in neurophysiology at a time when new technics became available to give impetus to fresh advancements in this century old field. Vacuum tube amplifiers were first used in the 1920's to study electrical messages in nerves. These tools were brought rapidly to technical fruition by the radio industry to satisfy public demands for Amos and Andy shows and jazz band programs. Here, applied science profoundly helped advance basic science—a reversal of the usual course of events. During the late 1920's and the 1930's, studies of the nervous system with these powerful analytical tools repeatedly turned up exciting new insights. For ten years I spent most of my time investigating messages in sensory nerves of animals and brain waves of animals and man. This work was done with a modest laboratory layout at Clark University where I held a professorship and with little in the way of technical assistance. These were years in which the a-ha phenomena occurred with pleasurable frequency.

As time went on answers to each question asked in the laboratory raised several new questions to be answered. I was tempted increasingly to apply for research grants to expand the scope of our activities. Thus it came to pass that assistants, students, and increasing administrative responsibilities took more and more time away from the laboratory bench. With these diversions the excitement of personally experiencing the a-ha phenomenon became somewhat less frequent, but the fact that my close associates were having such experiences produced vicarious satisfaction.

In 1938, Dr. Gregory Pincus joined my group at Clark University. We had been graduate students and later instructors together at Harvard. Pincus's work in the field of mammalian reproduction had been brilliant and he attracted grants to support his expanding program of activities. His interests came to involve problems of endocrinology. His concern with the role of sex hormones in mammalian reproduction led him on to fundamental discoveries in our laboratory about the role of the sex hormones in human cancer—discoveries which have had farreaching repercussions on cancer research.

I spent the summer of 1940 at the naval air training station at Pensacola with a group of physiologists and psychologists trying to devise better methods of selecting pilots. Some of us had the thought that electrical brain wave patterns might turn out to be diagnostic of flying ability. At the end of the summer it was clear that this hypothesis was of little value, but in my personal contacts with aviators I learned that flying military airplanes is very stressful and that fatigue of pilots was a pressing matter in relation to Air Corps operations.

In discussing this matter with Dr. Pincus, it seemed to us that perhaps hormones released from the adrenal cortex, the outside layer of the adrenal glands on top of the kidneys, might be involved in the problem and we accordingly set about investigating the role of the adrenal in fatigability with a group of volunteer Army pilots. To make a long story short, we did find that fatigue from flying is related to the response of the adrenal cortex. It was possible to correlate the fatigability of individual pilots with the output of urinary metabolites of the adrenal cortex hormones following the stress of flying. We also found that gradations of the response of this kind characterized the fatigability of factory workers, and in the course of our studies, we learned that this remarkable group of hormones are enhanced in their release by such diverse stresses as the taking of examinations, emotional factors, and the stress of operating industrial machines. In the early stages of this work we had only crude methods of estimating adrenal function but, as time went on, our laboratory and investigators elsewhere developed powerful technics for the analysis of the action of these hormones on important bodily processes. To do this, it was necessary to engage the services of chemists and physiologists and we found that our group continued to increase in size. In 1944, we had outgrown the available space at Clark University, which consisted of a barn that I rented as part of my living accommodations from the University and which had been converted to a laboratory to house our dozen workers.

Because of dissatisfaction with our working conditions at Clark, we decided on the radical expedient of asking friends to be trustees and incorporate for us a new nonprofit institution—the Worcester Foundation for Experimental Biology—with Dr. Pincus and me as co-directors. This institution has developed rapidly in the past seven years. Our Trustees bought an attractive country estate in a suburb of Worcester which was converted to a laboratory. Our staff has grown from twelve people in 1945 to one hundred in 1952, and we have built several new buildings to house our activities. We have no endowment or rich alumni and are supported entirely by research grants and annual gifts.

Once again, more by good luck than by good management, I was fortunate in entering early upon a field of research that in recent years has developed rapidly and has proved to be of considerable importance in the hands of many investigators scattered throughout the world. Everyone has heard of the substance cortisone which is one of the hormones from the adrenal cortex. This substance has farreaching repercussions on a number of disease conditions. ACTH, which is a hormone from the pituitary gland at the base of the brain, is the activating agent that makes the adrenal cortex synthesize and release its hormones. Since we early had become interested in the adrenal cortex, we were in a position to make contributions to a field which has during the past decade developed into one of the very important branches of medical science. The hormones of the adrenal cortex belong to the same chemical family as do the sex hormones with which Pincus and his collaborators had been concerned in cancer studies since the late 1930's so that a certain amount of technical knowhow was available to our group in our early ventures in the field of adrenal studies.

In the course of our investigations of human fatigue in relation to the adrenal cortex I had become impressed with the thought that certain patients in mental hospitals might show disturbances of excretion of hormones from this gland. Schizophrenic, or dementia praecox, patients are persons suffering from a very serious form of mental disease with a bad prognosis. These patients have notoriously failed to meet the stresses of living and have developed bizarre forms of behavior in response to these stresses. We asked ourselves whether we might find disturbances in the adrenal physiology for this group since we had observed the ubiquitous nature of adrenal responsivity to stress. For some ten years we have now investigated this problem with schizophrenic patients at the Worcester State Hospital and have found them to display interesting abnormalities in adrenal cortical function. Post-mortem examinations of schizophrenic brains have failed to show structural abnormalities related to the severe psychological disturbances. Consistent abnormalities of behavior patterns leading to a specific diagnosis must, however, have consistent abnormalities of physiological action correlated with them and since approximately twenty-five per cent of the hospital beds in the United States are occupied by these patients, the physical basis of this disorder is a very challenging one to investigate.

As a neurophysiologist I have studied the action of hormones from the adrenal cortex on the brain and we have found interesting relations of this group of substances to the brain physiology of animals. The schizophrenic patients, in contrast to normal people, show certain qualitative differences in their production of adrenal cortical hormones and also show on the average subnormal adrenal cortex response to stress and to injected ACTH. As a result of our work, leads concerning therapy have developed which are now under investigation, but the unraveling of the story has been a most complicated one from the biochemical point of view, as each year our chemists have developed newer and better methods of determining the pattern of output of hormones from the glands of human subjects.

Since the 1930's, when my work was concerned with studies of the physiology of nerves of animals, there has been a considerable change of emphasis in my professional life. Today, with a sizable organization of scientists investigating a number of aspects of biological problems ranging from cancer to mental disease in relation to a class of hormones, I have found myself less and less able to participate with my hands in the laboratory. This undoubtedly is no loss to the world but it is disturbing to me. I have been frustrated by this developing situation and have been appalled at the bright young men about me all of whom seem to know so much more than I do about so many technical things. I have often wondered if the development of a research foundation has been sufficiently internally satisfying in view of the loss of contact it has entailed with the details of scientific work. I have, however, concluded that I must have basically wished events to take this turn or they would not have done so. The combined output from a number of talented investigators which one has brought together is satisfying despite the personal frustrations that are involved in becoming a director rather than a performer.

For the professional scientist there is probably no one great moment of discovery. If he is productive, it is the frequency and magnitude of these moments which make him effective over the years.

I have liked Nevil Shute's preface to his play, *Vinland the Good,* in which he writes, "Some years ago I came upon the historical story of the discovery of America by Leif Ericson in A.D. 1003. I think this is one of the most fascinating adventures in history. This was no grandiose expedition of great people setting out in pomp and dignity from all the splendour of a Spanish royal court. This was a journey by the common man, a farmer, seeking to get a load of lumber to build cowhouses and discovering America on the side."

Many of the thrills of scientific discovery are the result of serendipity in the form of byproduct discoveries which come in the course of the routine investigation of a problem. The surge of imagination which sees new relationships of farreaching significance often disrupts organized programmatic research and planned research budgets, but it is just such surges developing in the minds of trained and disciplined observers that furnish the lasting personal rewards of the scientist and that have profoundly modified our way of life over the past three centuries.

II

THE JOY OF WORK AS PARTICIPATION

DOROTHY D. LEE

It was in a purely domestic situation that I had that moment of discovery of which I want to write now. It was on a Christmas Eve; I was working late at night, listening to the desultory talk of my husband and my brother-in-law. I was exhausted after a day of housework, of coping with two small children, of Christmas preparations; but I had to finish making bedding for a doll crib, and I was working against time, wishing I were in bed.

I had been living a life of conflict since my marriage, as I had felt that I owed it to my profession to continue my work in anthropology. This meant that I had to organize my life in such a way that my housewifely duties did not encroach unduly on my professional work; and I had to justify everything that I did as a housewife, as something which was imposed by the exigencies of my budget, or by my role as wife and mother. In this way, I did not need to feel guilty toward my profession. The doll blanket I was making that night was amply justified; it would give happiness to my three year old daughter and it had been necessary for me to take the time to make crib and bedding, for I could not afford to buy them.

As I sewed this Christmas Eve, I was suddenly astonished to discover that I had started to add an entirely unpremeditated and unnecessary edging of embroidery; and, simultaneously, I was aware of a deep enjoyment in what I was doing. It was a feeling that had nothing to do with the pleasure the work would give to my daughter on the morrow; it had nothing to do with a sense of achievement, or of

15

virtue in duty accomplished. And I know that I had never liked to embroider. There was no justification for my work; yet it was the source of such a deep satisfaction, that the late hour and my fatigue had ceased to exist for me. At this moment of discovery, I knew that I was experiencing what it meant to be a social being, not merely Dorothy Lee, an individual; I knew that I had truly become a mother, a wife, a neighbor, a teacher. I realized that some boundary had disappeared, so that I was working in a social medium; that I was not working for the future pleasure of a distant daughter, but rather in terms of my daughter, within a relationship unaffected by temporality or physical absence. What gave meaning to my work was the medium in which I was working—the medium of love, in a broad sense. My rationalization and justification of my work so far, had obscured this meaning, had cut me off from my own social context. It suddenly became clear to me that it did not matter whether I was scrubbing the kitchen floor or darning stockings or zipping up snowsuits; these all had meaning, not in themselves, but in terms of the situation of which they were a part. They contained social value because they implemented the value of the social situation.

This was a tremendous discovery for me, illuminating in a flash my experience and my thinking. My mind went immediately to the Tikopia, about whom I had been reading, and I said to myself, "This is the way the Tikopia work." I had been puzzled about the motivating forces in the life of the Tikopia. These were people without organized leadership in work, who yet carried out large undertakings; and without any authority to impose legislation and mete out punishment, the business of the village was carried out, and law and order were maintained. Raymond Firth, the ethnographer, spoke of obligations, duty, fear of adverse opinion, as motivations. I did not like his choice of words, because he spoke of the obligation to perform unpleasant tasks, for example, and yet the situations he described brimmed with joy. Now I saw that the Tikopia did not need external incentives.

This was all very well, but when I came to analyze my discovery, I could not explain it in any rational or acceptable way. My society did not structure working situations as occasions which contained their own satisfaction; and it assumed the existence of aggregates or collections of individuals, not of a social continuum. I had learned to believe in the existence of a distinct self, relating itself externally to work as a means to an end, with external incentives and external rewards. Yet it was obvious that if I got satisfaction from participating in a situation, there must be some medium, some continuum, within which this participation can take place. If my family and I were aspects of one whole, there must be some positive apprehension of a continuity which made me an aspect of my family, not a separate member; it was not enough to say that my physical being and my sensory experience did not in themselves prescribe the limits of the self.

And this is how I came to study the definition of the self among the Tikopia. It seemed to me that only on the basis of just such an assumption of continuity could their relations to man and nature and the divine, their words and phrasings and ceremonials be understood. I went back to Raymond Firth's books on the Tikopia, and read each detail without placing it automatically against my own conception of the self. And so I was able to see a conception of identity radically different from mine; I found a social definition of the self. I found that here I could not speak of man's relations with his universe, but rather of a universal interrelatedness, because man was not the focus from which relations flowed. I found a named and recognized medium of social continuity, implemented in social acts, not in words, and I found, for example, that an act of fondling or an embrace was not phrased as a "demonstration" or an "expression" of affection—*i.e.,* starting from the ego and defined in terms of the emotions of the ego—but as an act or moral supporter of comforting or of sharing—as a social act. I found a system of childrearing which trained in increasing interdependence and socialization, instead of training toward self-reliance and individuation. And here I found work whose motivation lay in the situation itself, a situation which included the worker and his society, the activity and its end, and whose satisfaction lay in social value.

What I say below, is based on three books by Raymond Firth, *We the Tikopia, Primitive Polynesian Economy,* and *The Work of the*

Gods, parts I and II. The interpretation is usually my own, based on intensive and detailed reading of this rich source of data.

Among the Tikopia, a newborn child is [1] not helped to recognize, discover, develop—or is it create?—his own separate identity; in fact, he is not treated as if he had such a separate identity. In my own culture, I had learned to speak of an infant as an "addition" to the family; and my planning for the coming baby had been in terms of something added. I found an additional room, additional furniture, and added implements; I took out an additional insurance policy. But Firth spoke as if the child were no such addition. He spoke of the "entrance" of the child into a family circle, and everything he subsequently described conveyed the impression of a swelling of this circle, of an enhancement of social participation and social good.

From birth on, among the Tikopia, the infant is gradually and systematically introduced to a widening circle. At first, he is in close contact with the mother, held and suckled and comforted when awake, in immediate cutaneous contact. Very soon, the female aunts and other older relatives share this close care of, or involvement in, the infant. Then the father and the older male relatives begin to nurse the child, seeking his companionship. More and more distant relatives now come, male and female; and the child is introduced to their society deliberately, so that his affection and dependence should be spread widely. At some point during this process, the child is also introduced to the companionship of youths and maidens and little children. The infant may be turned over to the care of a six year old brother, who will be seen carrying him around, nuzzling and playing with him, and otherwise showing his enjoyment of him. Adolescent boys and girls, exchanging flirtatious talk in the shade, may choose to hold an infant in their arms.

This is not merely a recognition of the dependence of the infant. It is an expression of the interdependence within the social unit, of the value of togetherness. Close and distant relatives leave their homes and their occupations to be with a little grandchild or niece or cousin several times removed; or to carry a young relative off for a visit, or

---

[1] I have taken over the tense which Firth uses in his writings. I do not know whether Tikopia society has changed in the past twenty years.

down to the beach where the men sit together talking. It is not for lack of babysitters that babies are taken along by their parents when they go gardening. Firth speaks of how a man, called away from the talk of men by his wife to stay with the baby, leaves the group with a sense of dignity, not of annoyance and interruption.

Many Tikopia parents go even further in widening the circle in which their children participate. They lend them out as "adhering" children to other households; and now the children are parts of two family circles, sharing the intimate details of living with either, at their choice. Older children or adults may be invited to become adhering brothers or sisters or other relatives.

The structure of life within the family rests on the assumption that there is social continuity, and that this is good. In our own society, where we assume individual identity, we keep the physical entities strictly separate; only in sexual relations do we allow physical mingling. We do not like to breathe the breath of others, and avoid even feeling the breath of others. We protect privacy with the sanction of health and sanitation; it is good to have a room of one's own and unhealthy to share it with five others. It used to be merely a question of enough fresh air; it has since been transformed into a question of mental health; whatever the sanction, it does ensure privacy. In our society, clothing separates mother and child; is it to protect each from the hazards of a sudden draft? It was 102°F in my hospital room when I was first allowed to hold my baby; yet both baby and mother were carefully swathed in cloth which kept them to that degree distinct. Clothing, in fact, guards everyone against cutaneous contact with others, except perhaps, at the beach. We have divided our benches into individual units; our seats in school, on the train, on the bus. Even our solid sofas, planned for social groupings, have demarcating lines or separate pillows to help individuals keep apart. But the Tikopia help the self to be continuous with his society through their physical arrangements. They find it good to sleep side by side crowding each other, next to their children or their parents or their brothers and sisters, mixing sexes and generations; and if a widow finds herself alone in her one room house, she may adopt a child or a brother to allay her intolerable privacy.

In our society, we protect ourselves from each other's secretions, in the interest of sanitation. Who but very young children would think of sharing toothbrushes? But among the Tikopia, people like to chew the half masticated betel wads of others; and these are passed with affection from older to younger, from brother to sister.

In the area of food, also, we erect a sanitary barrier around the individual. A mother is urged never to taste food she cooks with the same spoon which she uses for stirring; and this, even though the temperature of the food is such that it will kill any germs she might introduce from her mouth. The disgust aroused if she acts otherwise has actually nothing to do with sanitation, but comes from the thought that the mother's saliva might in this way be introduced into the food. And, of course, when it comes to the care of infants, the mother is urged to be even more careful. So machinery chews the baby's food into a mash, bottlewarmers and other mechanical devices bring the child's food to body temperature, boiling water sterilizes away the mother's tactile contact, bottles and cups and spoons separate the mother from the mouth of the child.

The Tikopia mother phrases all feeding as physical continuity. If she is not suckling the child, she maintains this continuity in some other way. She masticates the solid food herself, partly digesting it with her saliva, before bending down to put it into the baby's mouth with her lips, like a bird feeding its young. The water she gives the baby is also mixed with her saliva first and warmed with her own body warmth in her mouth, before it is given to the baby with her lips.

Something of this is carried on into the family meal—or rather household meal, for a number of other relatives often live in the house, or share the meal of the day. The older members are deliberately given portions too large for them, and the younger members portions too small, so that the elder can pass their leavings to the younger. It is not a question of neatly cutting off the portion one cannot eat, and putting it aside; the Tikopia use no tools other than their hands in eating. The leavings are passed on bearing the marks of the eaters' fingers, which, carefully licked clean, have slid down the side of the heap. And the guest from another district is given an enormous portion, so that he can have his own leavings to take to his home.

This is not the same as taking a gift from the storehouse; this is taking a share of a social occasion away with him.

Work among the Tikopia is also socially conceived and structured; and if a man has to work alone, he will probably try to take a little child along. In our culture, the private office is a mark of status, an ideal; and a man has really arrived, when he can even have a receptionist to guard him from any social intrusion to which he has not first given his private consent. Our kitchen planners, caught between ideals of privacy and efficiency, on the one hand, and the new teachings of child specialists, on the other, have not yet managed to introduce the child into the kitchen as anything much better than a necessary evil. To the Tikopia, an American kitchen, with the mother mainly concerned in having everything within reach and no one under foot, would be an atrocity. When they prepare the meal, after they have returned from their gardening and other food getting occupations, the whole household works together. Nothing is within reach, and children fill this gap, fetching and carrying and running errands. Father and mother, the unmarried aunt, the grandmother, the brother-in-law, all work together, firing the oven, scraping taro, grating coconut. One gets fiber for making a coconut strainer, another squeezes out the coconut cream, another is nursing the baby. While they wait for the food to bake, they carve cups out of coconut shell, or plait sinnet, or play. Jokes and anecdotes fly back and forth. No one apparently wants to be alone so as to concentrate or to work more efficiently.

The work situations which Raymond Firth presents always convey this joy and sheer satisfaction, at least to this reader. There seems to be no compulsion to work. Firth speaks of "obligations," probably to explain to his Western readers how it is that a man will work without external coercion of any sort. But we find the Tikopia often choosing these "obligations." For example, Firth tells how the husbands of the women married out of a family group have the obligation to fire and tend the ovens when this family group performs a public celebration. But more than once he speaks of the sons of these women, who are the guests of honor on such occasions, and who nevertheless choose to assume the role of their dead fathers and come instead as cooks; here is choice, not compulsion. People choose to make contributions to the donor during a great gift giving occasion, even though they are to participate in the occasion as recipients, whether they have made a contribution or not. People manage to discover obscure avenues of relationship which will enable them to assume such "obligations": and this means that they will have to get and prepare and plait sinnet, or dig and scrape taro, or get pandannus and beat it into bark cloth; it also means a fuller participation and involvement in the social situation.

In our own culture, we do have what we call cooperative undertakings, and we urge parents to plan cooperative work for the family. But these are proposed ultimately for the benefit of the individual, so that the end is a collective end, not a common end. It would be a mistake to see the Tikopia situation as a cooperative one. Cooperation, like altruism, presupposes our own definition of a discrete self.

In the use they make of kinship terms, also, the Tikopia define the individual socially. Kinship terms, of course, always do define the individual on a social basis, and, to my knowledge, they are present in all societies. But not everywhere are they used as they are used among the Tikopia. Here the personal name is rarely used. Brothers and sisters call each other by kinship terms, and parents call their children "son" and "daughter" when they do not have to specify. In addressing or referring to older people, when specification is necessary, the name of the dwelling is used, such as "mother's brother from ——," not the personal name.

In the kind of terms which they choose to use, the Tikopia show the extent to which they view the individual as social. It seems to be a common practice, for example, to refer to, or address a relative, not in terms of his relation to oneself, but in terms of his relation to a common relative, thus widening the circle, and bringing in another relation by implication. A child, speaking to his mother's brother, will probably refer to his father as "Your brother-in-law." A father may call out to his sons, "You brethren." A man may address his son-in-law as "You brother-in-law-linked (*i.e.,* related as brother-in-law) to my son" thus evoking a fourth relative. A man may call his father-in-law *grandfather*-linked, thus introducing his own child into the term.

And when non-kin speak of others who may be considered to be related to one another in however distant a manner, they often refer to them in terms of this mutual relationship, not in terms of who they are as individuals. For example, Firth tells of seeing two women going by, and asking who they were. The answer came: "They are father's-sister-linked" (they are a woman and her brother's daughter). Firth was asking for a definition of their identities; what he got was a completely social definition, and still did not know "who" they were. He adds that even when accepting the answer given he was left puzzled, because the relationship, when he finally worked it out, was so tenuous and obscure. Yet his informant chose this as the basis for his definition.

The individual is known also in terms of another definition. When he marries and is the head of a household, he and his wife are known by the name of their house plot. In fact, there is a continuity between land, fenua, and people which is evidenced in the use of the word. A man says, "My *fenua*, it is Tikopia," and he also says, "*Fenua* has made speech," and, "*Fenua* is many" (many people are present). *Fenua* is also used to refer to the placenta. This continuity with land-society has found expression, negatively and disastrously, in intense nostalgia during absence. Recruiting for plantation labor was prohibited in Tikopia when repeated experience showed that almost all the men died when away from home. On one occasion, the twenty men taken to Guadalcanal were absolved from all plantation work and allowed to fish all day by way of arousing in them an interest in life; but, in spite of this treatment, only one of the twenty survived to return to Tikopia. An attempt by the Melanesian Mission to send boys away to school in 1928 met with failure, and all three had to be sent back by the next boat.

The Tikopia are continuous with their dead society as well. Under the floor of their houses, or just outside beneath the eaves, dwell their dead relatives. The presence of the dead is taken for granted, and there is frequent communication with them. One long dead ancestor even became a Christian, as he happened to be inhabiting a living Tikopia at the time when this man was being baptized. A dead Tikopia who dwelt under the floor of Raymond Firth's house objected to the crowds who gathered when the ethnographer played the gramophone; and Firth had to give up this recreation. There may be merely a matter of fact awareness of the presence of the dead, or there may be specific contact in a dream, or through a medium. The land "belongs" to the dead, and is under their care; so that their descendants walk carefully and in awareness on the land of their fathers. When a social offence is perpetrated, such as an incestuous marriage, it is the dead relatives who punish the living. At the beginning of a meal, some food is flung casually at the graves of the dead relatives; and, in fact, the relationship throughout has the casualness of an assured continuity. When the definite presence of a dead one is desired, a man will ask a medium to bring him for a visit. On one such occasion, Firth reports that the man who had issued the invitation had started on some occupation by the time his dead nephew arrived; so he simply asked the medium to offer the dead some betel nut and to tell him that his host was too busy to chew it with him.

The deities of the Tikopia are their early dead ancestors; so these also are eventually their relatives. They are addressed as grandparents, in terms implying a more relaxed relationship than the term for father or father's sister. They are treated with the respect and concern with which relatives are treated. For example, Firth describes how an expert, repairing a canoe from which the three inhabiting deities had been removed lest they be disturbed by the disruption to their body, worked furiously against time, worried because the gods were being deprived of their body. It was a question of sympathy, not of currying favor. And with their gods, the Tikopia feel so comfortable, that they play jokes on even the highest of them.

I have spoken of affection, sympathy, concern. The Tikopia have one word which covers these concepts and similar ones: *arofa*. Grief, gratitude, moral support, pride in, appreciation of another, all these are also included under this term. In fact, this is the term for social warmth, the social emotion, the continuity of which I have been speaking. Arofa and the acts of arofa, exist only among people who are socially continuous, kin and people who have shared living over a period of time. A man does not speak of feeling arofa for his sweetheart; in fact, the correct marriage is phrased as a violent and hostile abduction from the arofa group, separating an individual away from it in the way a strand is removed from a cord. Later, however, there is arofa between husband and wife. A man dividing his property, his clubs and spears, sinnet belts and ornaments, among his sons and grandsons, feels that he will now be, "properly present" in his descendants; and such heirlooms are tau-arofa: bond-of-arofa.[2] Men and women wear tau-arofa of dead and living relatives: teeth, bored and suspended on a cord; hair made into a circlet, a waistcloth. Women in particular wear circlets made of the hair of sons or brothers or husbands or fathers. These are visible forms of arofa.

Arofa exists in concrete act, as the Tikopia say; and such acts are many. Whenever an individual is in a position of strain or crisis, arofa is shown by his relatives through physical contact. If a small child wanders away from his father and is frightened or hurt, he runs back to be held in his father's arms. When he is older, this same physical contact gives him comfort and support under similar circumstances. When a boy or girl appears for the first time at the sacred dances of Marae, male relatives on the mother's side crowd around the novice, shielding the dancer from the eyes of the curious, holding up his arms, going with him through the motions of the dance. When a Tikopia is ill, the mother's brother will come and offer his back as a support to the sick one, or holds him in his arms. A more inclusive group of relatives, representing the complete social unit, assembles thickly at a time of birth, marriage, death.

The continuity of the individual with the social unit is particularly in evidence during the rites of the Firing of the Ovens of Youth, when the operation of superincision is performed on the young boys who are being initiated into the society of men. Nowadays the operation is performed with a razor blade, but earlier a sharp shell was used; and, in any case, it is still a painful performance, particularly as the operator is often not expert and not sure. It is an introduction to the society of men, not an ordeal to try fortitude; and the whole procedure

---

[2] I have found no term in English which will convey the meaning of *tau*. Firth, faced with this predicament, uses the word, "linked," which, I think, implies even more strongly a prior separation. Consanguine and affinal kin, as well as certain forms of "property" are referred to with *tau*.

is imbued with arofa in so many specific ways, that, in the end, the boys are said not to feel pain at the time of the operation.

Preparation for the rites begins months before the occasion. From now on the coming rites color the life of the large group of kin. Gardens are planted because of the additional food needed, coconuts are used frugally with an eye to the coming rites. Sinnet is made into cords for gifts, mats are woven, bark cloth is beaten, the reef is dragged; the whole social unit is involved to a greater or lesser extent. A few days before the actual operation, the boy is invited to the houses of relatives. There he is given food and he is smeared with vermillion turmeric. At each household, a female relative gives him a new loincloth; he removes the one from around his loins, and gives it to her to tie around her neck, as an act of arofa. At this time, his relatives begin to practice the singing of dirges whose general theme is arofa. In the meantime, taro is being dug by groups of men, women, and children, food is being collected in a huge pile, and preparations are being completed.

On the day of the operation, the boy continues the visiting of relatives, who smear him with turmeric and give him new waistcloths as before. And from early morning on this day, the assembled relatives sing dirges, mourning the shedding of the boy's blood, the injury to his flesh. As one group finishes, another group takes up the mourning. Men wail and sob, beating their breasts, women cut themselves with knives and gouge their flesh with their nails. By this time, the relatives have laid the boy's pain on their own necks, they have injured their own flesh, they have wept and mourned for the pain and injury to the boy. And from early morning, those who have not mourned have been busy working for the great gift giving which is the main part of these rites. They have been plaiting sinnet, grating taro, peeling bananas, kneading, working together.

It is finally time for the operation, the occasion for all this. The boy is now carried into the house on the back of his mother's brother, where he is dressed in a new waistcloth by female relatives, and covered with beads and other valuables. Now his uncle carries him to the place of operation, and sits holding him in his arms. Around them presses the group of near relatives, body close against body, giving support in this period of crisis. A general wailing has begun when the boy was brought to the house, and now the women are crying gently. Everyone has wailed and mourned, except the boy. His pain, his fear, his injury have been shared by all, diffused in time and in space through the arofa of his group.

There is no song of rejoicing now that the operation is over; there is no singling out of the boy. If there is any feeling of achievement, it is that of the leader of the rites, who says, "Our work is good, let us sit and chew betel." From now on, the group plunges into an intricate series of gift giving situations, which, according to Firth, are the most important event of the day. The boy, on this important day when he receives this painful mark of his initiation into the status of manhood, has furnished merely the occasion for a particularly intense and prolonged social participation. Now comes an extensive web of contributions to the main gift which has been prepared by many people over a period of months. There are gifts and countergifts, according to established structure, until everyone has had an active share in the great gift giving occasion. As the mats and barkcloths are received, the boy is made to lie between them; subsequently, these will be distributed to every household, carrying with them some contact with the boy. In this and other ways, the boy comes eventually in touch with his whole social unit on this occasion. Yet he is not the focus of these rites; there is no focus.

Such are the occasions marking the new status which comes from an introduction into the widening circle of adult society; in their function, they may be compared to commencement in our society, or to the Bar Mitzvah. No individual achievement is celebrated; though many gifts are given and received, none are given to the boy himself and for himself, except for the transient flow of loincloths. Before the incision rites, another occasion has been celebrated in a mild way in the growing boy's life; this was his first experience of torchlight fishing. At this time, no one is concerned with the boy's achievement, and in fact he has achieved nothing except joining a crew. He is not even given a torch to hold or a net to use. He merely paddles with the rest of the crew; and it is this step in increasing socialization which is marked with a firing of the ovens, and a gift giving. Social development, not increased individuation, is celebrated and the only gift given to the boy is one which he is to take to his parents.

Society appears as the referent in other ways. The commonest curse, used casually and without offense, is a "social" one: "May your father eat filth." Even fathers use this to their children. Birth control and infanticide are carried on in the name of society: so that there should be enough for all. Gift exchanges are carried on in such a way that everyone in the unit participates in giving; until time runs short, gifts from a household are announced in the names of all, even the young children. If some giver's name is omitted by some oversight, some relative may whisper to have one of his gifts announced in the name of the slighted giver, so that this man, too, can have a share in the occasion.

It is with such a definition of the self, and such a conception of work as taking place within a medium of arofa, of social continuity, that work occurs among the Tikopia, without coercion, without the incentive of reward or fear of punishment, without the spur of individual profit; work is an occasion containing meaning because it is a part of a social situation with which the individual is continuous.

III

DISEASE AND THE PATTERNS OF BEHAVIOR

HAROLD G. WOLFF, M.D.

It is my purpose to select, from a quarter century of bedside and laboratory experience, those "moments of discovery" which served to indicate a path, however indistinct, rather than those that momentarily fiercely lighted my feet.

Like many others before me, I have rediscovered that the perception of an order in the universe is for man a moralizing experience. The more inclusive the arrangement, the more moving is the spectacle. Especially is this so if the order perceived concerns man directly. The exploration of man's relation to the universe, and especially of man's nature, is thus an endlessly life-giving pursuit. Whether one orients oneself to such order in theistic or humanistic terms, becomes, in the main, a matter of esthetic preference.

I would like to start with some studies on pain. We early discovered, much to our surprise, that all human beings have the same threshold; the point at which they first perceive pain is the same for all persons. Indeed, my colleague, Dr. Hardy, just back from regions near the North Pole, worked with Eskimos, and found their pain thresholds to be the same as ours. We found also, that there are a limited number of discriminable steps between the point at which pain is first perceived and the point beyond which discriminations are impossible.

However, what one does with such pain perception is extremely variable. It soon became apparent that it did not make much difference what the nature of the damaging influence was; whether much or little was made of this painful sensation seemed to depend more upon the individual and his background than upon the intensity of the stimulus.

It also became apparent that man, constituted as he is, was capable of responding in much the same way to tissue damage—which is, after all, the basis for the painful sensation—and to symbols or threats of danger. And, interestingly enough, the responses to pain, tissue damage, or to the symbols of tissue damage—to threats, in other words—were often more destructive than were the effects of the damaging agent.

The next step in our observations had to do with the fact that man, being a tribal animal and so much dependent upon the support and encouragement of his group, is jeopardized by their disapproval and much taken up with his fear of being incapable of carrying on as a man. Such environmental forces, representing the impact of man on man, being ubiquitous, constitute one of his greatest threats. This led us to extend our studies beyond those on pain as a sensation and the reactions to tissue damage. We began to analyze the brigade of human reactions to threats and symbols of danger—epitomized in what man does to man; we studied his attitudes, the conflicts his goals engender, and the price he pays for his achievements.

Let me illustrate by example. If someone strikes your forearm with a ferrule, the skin will become red, and after a while, if the blow has been forceful enough, a wheal, or a whitened, elevated area will appear. The latter represents the lack of capacity of the small blood vessels in the skin to hold on to their bloody contents, and some of them leak out into the tissue, and, in a sense, protect for the moment that area of skin against further injury.

If after such an experience, and as a sham blow, that ferrule is brought down to within an inch of the arm, the skin behaves very much as if it had been struck, although there has been no actual damage done. Reaction to the threat, therefore, is like that to the blow.

Let us now consider a person with hives—large swollen areas of the skin, with various technical names. Out of the medley of information gleaned from a survey of the subject's major interests, relations and past, pertinent topics were selected that were potentially traumatic. When that individual was then confronted by and contemplated such topics, he exhibited in his skin the same reaction as he did under circumstances when his skin was actually struck. The reaction to a variety of traumatic agents was found to be the same. Also, the reaction to a symbol or a threat of assault was repeatedly observed to be the same as that to the assault itself.

The individual, when asked what he feels under these circumstances, if articulate, may say, "I feel as though I were taking a beating and that I can do nothing about it."

We interested ourselves in the stomach because complaints from the abdomen and from the head constitute, in the physician's ears, the bulk of human complaining.

We were much helped by a man who came into our circle of friends and workers. He was at that time about sixty-five, and as a child of nine, had occluded his gullet by drinking scalding hot clam chowder. Thereafter, he had to be fed through a hole made in his abdomen. Becoming as he did, a part of our laboratory family, he allowed us to examine every day what was going on in this hole in his abdomen. He also allowed us to try to relate the overall circumstances of his life, the way he felt about them, with what we saw as regards blood flow, the amount of secretion, and the motility of the stomach. It was his custom to come to us each morning, having fasted after his evening meal. He would narrate, and we would observe and note.

A characteristic situation and reaction was one such as this: his income as a university employee was small, and in order to swell it, he took on the task of dusting the apartment of an associate. He was not a good housekeeper and was indifferent about dust. My associate wished to dismiss him and finally did so under laboratory circumstances. While he was being denounced by his employer and told of his ineffectiveness as a worker, the mucous membrane lining of the stomach became fiery red, large amounts of digestive juices were secreted, and his stomach began to churn. Subsequently, when my colleague left, the subject said, "I'd like to wring his neck."

Now, what did we see? We saw exactly what we would have seen had we placed some attractive, palatable food into this man's stoma. Here was a man angered by another man, whose stomach acted under these circumstances as if he were preparing to eat! Why do we use an eating pattern when we are angry? To be sure, this is not universal, but under certain circumstances, feelings of anger are associated with a preparation for eating. If this preparation for eating goes on (as it can) for days, weeks, or months, the individual may digest his own digestive apparatus; he bores a hole, so to speak, in the lining of his stomach.

We have now considered two examples of the inappropriate use of protective or adaptive patterns. A city man cannot "eat" his enemy; he cannot minimize the effects of an unfriendly remark by any protective action within his skin. And yet, maintaining such patterns for days, weeks, or months at a high intensity may seriously damage organs and parts. Not because they were originally weak. Indeed, they may have been strong; but they are damaged because of prolonged and excessive use of structures not designed to meet such needs.

The digestive equipment exhibited an ejection pattern when a zealous young Jewess was confronted by an incident indicating to her that Zionists were being persecuted. She reacted with feelings of disgust and her stomach took on the pattern which the word, "disgust," suggests, namely, faulty digestion. The contents of the stomach were ejected just as though she had taken in some poison.

The pattern of dealing with disgusting behavior on the part of man was the same as that evoked by putting ipecac or a "disgusting" tasting material into the mouth.

Later, we were fortunate in being able to study four individuals who, for surgical reasons, had to have parts of their large intestine exposed to the outer world. Again we could correlate from hour to hour, day to day, and month to month the life circumstances, the feelings aroused by threats and delights, and the change in the large bowel. Likewise, we found that if we put irritant substances into the bowel, say, croton oil, the mucous membrane got red, mucus poured out, the gut became hypermotile, and soon this irritant was pushed out of the gut.

One of these unfortunate men, following the death of his mother, became the nominal head of his household. A timid, shy person, he was unprepared for the position of family authority. He felt himself challenged when his brother's wife came into the household to live and because of her temperament, began to dominate him and the situation. Humiliated and angered, his discussion of this topic caused the lining of his gut to become fiery red, pour out secretions, and become hypermotile. Under these circumstances, the slightest injury, ordinarily sustained with indifference, caused hemorrhage. He repeatedly bled from his bowel and, as an end-picture, exhibited ulcerative colitis, following the inappropriate use of a pattern design to meet the special circumstances of a poisonous substance on its surface. He was using this pattern to get rid of a situation which could never be got rid of in that particular way.

The nose affords an easy opportunity for examination because it is always available and the contents of the airways are clearly in view. When one sits before a subject, holding an irritant substance such as smelling salts, and allows these fumes to ascend into his nostrils, the mucous membranes get red, become swollen, secretion pours out, the airways become obstructed and narrow; the diaphragm goes into cramp and breathing becomes impossible for a moment. The individual presents the pattern of shutting out, washing away, and neutralizing a dangerous environmental gas.

There came to us a woman who had had endless nose difficulties, for which she had undergone many operations. Although unhappily married, she never fully expressed her dissatisfaction. Nor did she fully assume her responsibilities as a wife and a mother. When confronted by the suggestion that her nose troubles might have been related to her attitudes and to the situation in which she found herself, the mucous membranes of the airways acted just as though she had inhaled a noxious gas. They became red, swollen, wet, and obstructed the passage of air. She attempted to shut out, neutralize, and wash away a set of circumstances that could never be so dealt with—another inappropriate use of a pattern.

Coming back to the theme, "moments of discovery," and the order that they reveal, I offer you these patterns: patterns integrated not by any one part of the nervous system, or any one structure or endocrine organ, but representing overall reactions of an individual to threats.

Seldom do substituted patterns effectively work for one, except incidentally. Thus, weeping under humiliating circumstances does not right a wrong, yet the fulfilment of the weeping pattern often makes us feel more comfortable.

All loads, or threats, dangerous though they be, do not evoke the same responses. Why does one person behave in one way, and another behave in a different way? Why does one man use his stomach, another his bowel, another his heart, another his head?

Perhaps that is not a fair question to ask of Nature, any more than to ask why the retriever dog more readily retrieves than the Boston bull, or why the beaver builds dams, whereas the squirrel collects nuts.

Patterns run in stocks, and a man may come of a "stomach family," of a "head family," or a "heart family."

I repeat, situations have no universal significance and evoke quite different responses in different people, and even in the same individual at different times.

Some penetrating observations in this regard were made by the professor of medicine, Dr. J. Groen, at the University of Amsterdam, who, being a Jew, was able to care for certain Jewish merchants in Amsterdam before and after the German occupation. These prosperous, successful citizens had in common the disorder known as ulcers of the stomach. They weathered the days of starvation with the Dutch without either strikingly good or bad effects on their digestive function. Ultimately, they were put into concentration camps and indeed their lives were then gravely threatened. No one knew when he awakened in the morning whether he would survive that day.

They were separated and deprived in many ways; they were filled with hatred—often enough for their own groups of different nationalities: the Dutch hated the Polish, the Polish hated the French, etc. They fought and snarled and sneered and snatched. They maintained no standards; fought for no banner of human ethic; they merely attempted to survive the day.

Yet during that time those men lost all signs of ulceration of their stomachs. Here were people who were exposed to great trouble and yet they lost the bodily disorder engendered by civil life. Ironically enough, they regained it when after the war they returned to "Main Street" and pursued their civilian goals.

In brief, man's mucous membranes, participating as they do in his bodily reactions to man's impact on man, may exhibit engorgement, ischemia, hemorrhage, edema, erosion, modification in secretion, ulceration, altered reaction to chemical agents, modification of cellular components and inflammation, with lowering of the pain threshold. Such alterations may become the basis of further and, in some cases, irreversible tissue damage with the well known manifestations of "organic" disease.

To continue then with the consideration of the meaning of a situation, let me cite as evidence a group of missionaries in Korea, ostensibly successful in their work, but who suffered frightfully with headache. During their incarceration in Japanese prison camps, deprived and threatened as regards their very lives, this group lost their headaches entirely. When at the end of the war they were able in many instances to return to this country and resume parish work or teaching, headaches returned.

In other words, threats are perceived differently and individually, and depending on what they mean, they evoke one or another adaptive or protective response.

Many headaches result from the improper use of the muscles of the head and neck, muscles that would ordinarily be used in preparing for action which, in these persons, is not perpetrated. Headaches also result from the engorgement of blood vessels on the outside and in the inside of the head; often such headaches occur in individuals who look at life in special terms. The man with headache, wishing "to get something done," drives himself "against time," is persistent, meticulous, order-loving, insistent on promptness, impatient of defects in himself and others, pushes himself to limits beyond his capacity, ultimately depletes himself and then starts a painful chain of events. In a comparable way, the person with hives feels as though he were "taking a beating"; the individual with the peptic ulcer is angered at mistreatment or the deprivation of his needs; the individual with the ulcerated bowel feels as though he would like to get rid of a menace; the individual with the obstructed nose wishes to avoid "taking part." A man vomiting at the side of a dead child run over by him in his automobile, may say, if articulate, "Oh, if only it had never happened" —a reaction to the situation as if he could deal with it by ejection, an act of riddance. These patterns so useful in themselves, are inappropriately used in each instance.

These orderly arrangements represent adaptive patterns involving portals of exit and entry. However, there are patterns that involve the circulation and general mobilization equipment. So may be viewed the response of the man with high blood pressure who is meeting an emergency by being alert and ready for any danger, a bodily response which is never actually put into proper use. Such an individual is poised, collected, ostensibly calm, but in reality, is alerted in readiness for an action which is never carried out. His response illustrates again the prolonged, inappropriate use of adaptive devices designed for short-time service.

Again, the end of such inappropriate use is "organic" disease: the heart overworks, the blood vessels to important organs constrict, parts run short of nourishment, the blood becomes sticky and coagulates too readily, the head aches severely, the muscles of the back "cramp." Let me then epitomize what I have tried to impart: man is capable of reacting to threats as though to assaults; that in so doing he inappropriately uses, over long periods, patterns designed for short-term and phasic actions, and to no end that they can meet; in so doing, he damages himself and threatens survival.

Along with these bodily changes, complaints of discomfort, of pain and suffering are uttered. Feelings and behavior are altered concomitantly. He may be frankly anxious and exhibit it; he may turn his fears into meticulous actions of perfectionism and excessive orderliness and promptness. He may blame others for those things that have gone wrong with his life. He may withdraw into himself and imply, "I am superior to all this and nothing can do me harm"—a resolution that may end in disaster. And, most conspicuous in our time, and for whatever reason, are feelings of guilt.

What then does this perception of an order represent? For review I have picked out from an apparent chaos of fortuitous responses, sequences which are destructive, but fit into patterns full of meaning. They challenge us to see man in his inner character and his place in nature. Also, in increasing understanding, we are encouraged to seek a way out of such perverse use of our endowments.

The important aspect of these experiences is not whether they "have registered" in the "conscious" or the "unconscious," but what threatening significance a given event has to an individual. Often significant events and relationships of a threatening nature, because of their ubiquity and the distress they create, are "pushed out of awareness," and evidences of their effects may be found in the "unconscious" if the search be made. But it is to be emphasized that often they may be found in the conscious, too, and be as destructive.

Again, it is of less concern whether the conflicting elements from an experience, or the unpleasant feeling state be "conscious" or "unconscious," but more the degree to which the individual at the time perceives his danger and can operate in terms of the threat. True, much of experience falls out of memory or consciousness and therefore is seemingly lost to us, and lost to us especially from the point of view of willful operation and correction. Yet, despite this incomplete awareness, we often "muddle through" (perhaps painfully); sometimes when these matters are brought to the surface, we are able to come to grips with them more effectively.

The human environment has much to do with this, and the stability of society is relevant. A most dangerous feature of man's experience is rapid and violent change.

Nearly twenty-five centuries ago Hippocrates reminded his contemporaries of the risks of change when he said, "Those things which one has been accustomed to for a long time, although worse than things which one is not accustomed to, usually give less disturbance. . . ."

A striking and relevant observation was made upon Hopi Indians. The young Hopi Indian, American schooled, may be contrasted with his father. His father believed that when he trod upon the track of a snake he would experience sore ankles unless he took himself to the medicine man, who, having the know-how, would rid him of the risk of sore ankles. This he unquestioningly believed, and acting so, his sore ankles were prevented. In contrast, his American schooled son, treading upon the track of a snake, no longer believing in the powers of the medicine man, considering him a "fake," a "phony," a "humbug," nonetheless experiences sore ankles.

The implication is clear. In a rapidly changing society, the anxiety-inducing factors (society decrees it is dangerous to step on the track of the snake because the snake may be nearby) are carried along in the traditions of a society and outlive the anxiety-resolving factors, namely, in this instance, the capacity of the medicine man to free the individual of the consequences of his transgressions.

We live in a rapidly changing society, in an environment where anxiety-inducing features outlast the devices for resolving them. Few institutions survive under these circumstances, and those that do are strained. Among the latter are marriage and the patient-physician relationship. We well know that the marital relationship is showing evidence of the strain. The patient-physician relationship is also pressed because the physician is reluctant, and often unable, to assume the responsibilities formerly spread over many institutions.

What is the evidence that these factors are relevant to disease? It is no accident that ulceration of the stomach, predominantly a woman's disease in the middle of the nineteenth century, occurring then about three to one in favor of women, has now become, in the middle of the twentieth century, with the many changes in the man-woman relationship, a man's disease to the extent in some areas of 12–16 to 1.

It is no accident that tuberculosis mortality reaches its peak within ten to twenty years of the industrialization of a society and thereafter rapidly falls off. It is no accident that when populations are moved, troubles ensue. When an Irish population emigrated to a new environment in American seacoast cities, despite the fact that people were better fed, had more opportunities, were titillated, and had more promise for the future, the mortality from tuberculosis among the Irish in New York City, for instance, was one hundred per cent greater than it was at the same time in Dublin.

It is no accident that the American Indians, moved from the plains to reservations, geographically not very far distant, exhibited a great increase of tuberculosis; or that the Bantu natives, removed from the country outside of Johannesburg into the environs of the city, died of tuberculosis in great numbers. Some, knowing they were about to die, asked to be brought back to their kraals. Many died; a few recovered, but tuberculosis was widely spread in the native villages. Interestingly, mortality from tuberculosis did not vastly increase with such spread, suggesting that the natives in their proper environment could deal with the infection.

It is no accident that the incidence of Graves' disease, or hyperthyroidism, in Norway, increased one hundred per cent during the first year of World War II when that country was invaded.

I am not discouraged by this sad story because we begin to learn what price we pay for our goals; that disease is indeed related to our attitudes, our individual and group actions, our goals, and the conflicts they engender.

There are values far more important than the avoidance of discomfort, pain, illness; and occasionally even individual survival is not important. There is strength in this knowledge. We begin to know the price we pay for a way of life. We need to accept personal limitations and be willing to deal with the consequences of our acts. But a man should appreciate what his actions and goals are costing him. Then, if he chooses, he may pay for them in pain and disease. Often he will decide that his values are poor, that he has been confused, and thereon changes his direction and pace.

All of these elementary facts we have relearned. These "moments of discovery" touched upon so lightly here have reemphasized what has long been known: that the impact of man on man may be as catastrophic as earthquakes, volcanic eruptions, and micro-organisms. On the other hand, it is also clear that much of the mischief, being manmade, can be undone by men who, speaking with the voice of authority, can encourage, teach, and assuage guilt.

IV

AFTER DISPLACEMENTS I FIND COHERENCE AGAIN

BY

STEPHEN S. KAYSER

Wherever we use the word, "incident," we can replace it with the word, "necessity"; it depends only on the general philosophy of life to determine which one of the two words one chooses. To see the hand of destiny everywhere seems as inconsistent with daily experiences as it is distressing to look upon everything as casually occurring by mere chance. There is a medium road in the interpretation of life and the world; it refuses to accept everything as predestined and yet does not overlook the benefit of adding meaning and purport to whatever occurs to us and around us. A landscape is not a part of nature, because "landscape" as such does not exist. Yet this does not prevent the artist from selecting a part of it which he places within the confines of his canvas, adding his own mood to the shapes and colors he sees. He has given form to something which had no coherence before. He changes it, yet at the same time he achieves a similarity on a different level.

Each one of us can give form to his life. As it passes by, day after day, it can well be drowned in the "moments" of which time consists. But if we can shape it by searching for its meaning, we rise above each momentary pettiness and bring into it something which is not just the summation, but the integration of particles of time. We can do this by "taking stock" now and again. We may then discover the integrating force which molds our lives. The discoveries which we make at these certain moments and which may so strongly dictate our further course can be termed "Voice of Destiny" or, more modestly, "Calls to Duty." Thereby the word, "moment," is to be understood not as a small segment of time, but rather in its original Latin meaning, as a momentum, an impetus to move in a particular direction. On the following pages instead of moments of discovery, I may in retrospect speak rather of the discovery of certain moments.

I was brought up in the old house of my grandfather in the southern German city of Karlsruhe, the somewhat sleepy capital of the Grand Duchy of Baden. It was an idyllic town, of classicistic simplicity. The only architectural disgrace in the beautifully planned inner city was the police department building which disturbed the harmony of the marketplace in a typical outburst of subordinating magistracy. Because of family relations of the rulers, the Grand Duchy of Baden was the only state in southern Germany which imported staff sergeants from Prussia for the training of its troops. These were the outer signs of gradual enemy occupation which was finally completed in the Hitler movement.

I am a firm believer in the two Germanies, one of the spirit and the other of power: one which embraced mankind, and the other which glorified the goose step. The latter is at present only handicapped; the other has vanished in time or in space.

Southern Germany was only reluctantly brought into the Prussian dominated Reich of 1871. Since the Emancipation, no antiSemitic movement originated there before 1919. The Jews of southern Germany, particularly those living in small communities, were a part of their surroundings. True enough, the wife of Berthold Auerbach, rabbinical student, writer, and novelist, was killed in an antiSemitic outburst in Heidelberg. But that happened in the stormy year of 1848. Auerbach himself is a typical example of the mentality of the Jew in southern Germany. He is no longer remembered as the author who published *The Ghetto,* dealing with Jewish life in the age of Moses Mendelssohn, but as the writer of the *Tales of the Black Forest Villages* which skillfully portray the peasant life in that mountainous region. Friedrich Nietzsche admired them greatly. During the Franco-Prussian War, Auerbach worked in the headquarters of the Grand Duke of Baden where he drew up proclamations. He was convinced then that antiSemitism was dead, and when it raised its ugly head again—typically enough, it was at that time named the "Berlin Movement"—Auerbach called it "the nail to my coffin."

When the story is written of the Jews in the small towns and villages of southern Germany from the beginning of the past century, it will show their roots strongly planted in the soil of the land, in conjunction with a fervent feeling for Jewish tradition colored by many superstitions which proved the lack of spiritual leadership. In this atmosphere, the miracle worker, Seckl Loeb Wormser, known as the Baal Shem of Michelstadt, rose to fame. In this world of wonder healings, exorcisms, and magic practices, my grandfather had grown up before he came to the city. Although I was a small child when he died, he left a lasting impression upon me. Many superstitious practices survived in his house. The life of a child in a strictly observant family underwent severe tests when the orthodox observances conflicted with the practices of the outside world. American children enjoy the blessing of not going to school on Saturday; it was different across the seas. Sabbath morning there meant going to public school, but in my case, not writing, while some Jewish schoolfellows did write on the sacred day. In grammar school, the difficulties were not too great, but in the classical state school, those master educators called professors could ask peculiar questions.

I remember how one of these gentlemen who chased us through the jungles of Latin grammar, interrogated me once about whether I considered myself a better Jew because I did not "work" on the Sabbath—he called it laziness—while other Jewish boys performed their "duty." It was the day when the declination of the word, *"homo,"* was taken up and the example in the book read: *"Homo homini lupus"* (Man is a beast to man). How true!

This type of teacher was another incarnation of Prussianized Germany. In many cases he was a *"Reserve-Offizier,"* a class who mentally never left the barrackyards, ill qualified to interpret the humanistic ideals of Greece and Rome for which they had to lay the grammatical foundations. My Christian classmates were generally not like the majority of the teachers, and in some cases true friendship developed. Only once a year did I feel a certain antagonism—around Easter time, when the story of the Crucifixion was told in religious instruction.

In the two entirely different worlds in which I lived, the synagogue was not only a house of worship and learning; it became a haven of mental refuge. To me, the visible community of worshipers became a source of strength, much more so than the Jewish youth movement which I had joined. When the Hitler deluge overcame us, the religious force built up in early years was the strongest antidote. The hours we spent in the houses of worship while the arm of the Gestapo threatened to catch each and everyone of us, were unforgettable experiences of fateful fellowship, welded together in the sacred traditions of our people. The discoveries of my youth regarding the elements of Nazidom latent in the average German now appeared magnified a thousandfold. It was nothing new. But that seemed unimportant in comparison to the inner resistance whose foundation had been laid in my Jewish upbringing. What I had felt at an early age, had become evident: there was no fusion possible between the German and the Jewish worlds into which I was born. Yet, there was still another realm where the commandos of the barrackyards became silenced and the horizon widened into the universal meaning of beauty and the spirit. I was not quite twelve years of age when I discovered the entrance into that world which from that time on drew me more and more into the orbit of its noble attractions. It happened by mere coincidence when, because I had hurt myself while cleaning my bicycle one Sunday morning, I was pacified by being allowed to go to the opera on my mother's ticket. Of all things, I heard Mozart's *Don Giovanni*. From the first notes of the overture to the turbulent finale—the charming reappearance of the ensemble without the villainous hero in front of the curtain was omitted in the court theater—I felt captivated. In this profound musical phantasy there was a magic challenge of which I wanted to know the secret.

I searched for the door of understanding. Soon I found that there was ample literature at hand, biographies of the composers, introductions to the score, which at first confused more than enlightened me. But I kept on with my search for understanding and, when soon afterward I went to the same opera again I was amply rewarded for the arduousness of those first searching steps. I had found a rich and fascinating world.

The war of 1914 did not touch it very much at first, although sounds of cannons from afar soon changed into the explosion of bombs from French airplanes in terribly close vicinity. The ending year of the war found me in the uniform of a foot soldier. By that time, I wanted to understand understanding itself, and so I became a student of philosophy.

After the war I wanted to go to the University of Heidelberg. My first acquaintance with this noble place of learning was almost symbolic. In 1916, Martin Buber came from his neighboring residence in Heppenheim to read from his Hassidic stories. The event took place one evening in one of the large lecture halls of the University, where I would in later years listen to the historian, Hermann Oncken. It was midsummer. The pale, bearded face of the reviver of the Baal Shem and the Great Maggid was lit by the gloomy bulbs of the antiquated lecture hall in the parting hour of the day, when suddenly a thunder storm came up, sending a blast of wind through the auditorium.

Buber was the one who showed me—as he did many of my generation—the connection between the spiritual world around us and the Jewish heritage in us, through the living method of his equation of man and Jew. My adolescence would have been spared many painful conflicts and experiences had his teaching been able to lay a spiritual foundation to the laws of tradition. Perhaps there is no philosophy which in itself can justify the necessity for doing things in accordance with religious precepts. The act of complying comes first. Yet, if the underlying principles are endangered from one side by spiritual forces, it needs other forces of that kind to reestablish the balance. And those counteracting weapons I could not find sufficiently strong in the Buber arsenal.

Never will I forget those months of hope—only months, not years—after the ending of the First World War. They seemed like the dawn of a new day when the Germany of the spirit could rise again. Although this hope vanished only too soon, at least its memory was left and it accompanied me throughout the years of study at Heidelberg, when it seemed at first that the reactionary forces were in the minority among the faculty. All too soon the picture changed. Even in the lectures on physics one could hear antiSemitic outbursts by the professor. And yet, for a decade, the name of Heidelberg was also connected with that of Friedrich Gundolf and everything that he stood for.

My teacher, Heinrich Rickert, never concealed the fact that he did not feel at ease in the German Republic, although his father once was an ardent democrat and he himself had every reason to be satisfied. I am indebted to him, aside from a thorough training in the field of systematic philosophy, for insight into the realm of esthetics. It was mainly under his influence that I became more and more interested in the visual arts for which Heidelberg offered two outstanding teachers, Ludwig Curtius, the archeologist, and Carl Neumann, the biographer of Rembrandt. In addition to these two, the philologist, Franz Boll, with his farreaching interpretations of the spirit of antiquity and his works on ancient astrology, provided me with guiding principles for which I still feel indebted to my Alma Mater.

Once we asked Professor Boll to give a lecture course on Homer's *Odyssey*. He said that he would do so only after he had seen the Mediterranean again. Soon afterward I had a chance to see that coast of Italy myself. Only then did I fully comprehend what Boll had meant regarding the inspiration of the atmosphere in which a work of art originates. Never did I understand the work of Michelangelo better than after I had seen the marble quarries of Serravezza and Pietrasanta where the sculptor himself had gathered the blocks out of which he carved his great works. Thus the years of apprenticeship and travel were enriched by lasting impressions and experiences. Fortunately my activities as an art critic and editor provided many opportunities for travel.

Once I had to report on an exhibition by a woman artist. I was impressed by the certainty of the brushstroke, the vivid coloring, and the emotional strength expressed in her canvases. One, particularly, showing a white house at Lugano, attracted my attention. The white wall placed in dark trees reflected not only the outer appearance of southern light, but a strong and loving soul as well. The artist not long afterward became my wife. Thus the first conflict which had arisen in my youth, the cleavage between the creative and the contemplative approach to the arts, was overcome in a way which I could not anticipate. Now I lived with the process of creation. During more than two and one half decades, this nearness to the productive force of art became the source of an ever closer cooperation. Hardly could we know that it would finally lead us to a common task in which we both realize the fulfilment of our early dreams. Thus the inspiration which struck me while gazing at an oil painting became the happiest and most important discovery of my life.

The biblical Book of Proverbs, a source of profound wisdom, contains one sentence to which I have always attached great significance: "Death and life are in the power of the tongue" (18:21). According to ancient belief, of two alternatives the preferable one shall be mentioned last. That is why the proverb quoted speaks first of death. I was to experience the full depth of the meaning of that biblical saying. My main instrument of expression was the German language. The very thought of having to express something in any other tongue was equal to abandoning the effort. During the years preceding Hitler's rise to power, the awareness of the limitations of one's native language as the only means to make a living became frightening.

There were too many straws in the wind not to see what was afoot. After Nazidom had finally become victorious, I chose Czechoslovakia as a country of immigration because the German language was still spoken by one-third of its population. So I taught the history of art in the Moravian capital of Brno. To live, not just to travel, in a bilingual country—actually in some parts of Czechoslovakia four languages are spoken—is a challenging experience. There were ample discoveries to make, particularly about the cultural achievements of the Slavs, of which the Czech nation reaches farthest west into the Germanspeaking orbit. In spite of the strong nationalism, understandable after three centuries of Hapsburg rule, I could see the important role this people played in the mediation between the East and West. Its tragic fate, trodden down under the heels of Bolshevism, can most keenly be felt by those who have lived there and witnessed the courageous struggle of the Czech for cultural values in a true democratic sense. I am convinced that the Czechs will be the first amongst the enslaved Slavs to cast off the yoke of spiritual and physical oppression.

The better I came to know the Czech spirit, the more I realized that the boundaries of one's language begin to crumble as soon as one discovers it to be just one instrument of expression among others. I began to feel more independent of my native tongue when, at the same time, I realized more and more that the fate of Europe was doomed and that Hitler was determined to conquer the entire continent, especially after having received so many indirect invitations to do so from the Western powers.

Three months before Munich, I came to the United States. Again, I asked myself, shall death or life be in the power of the language? My love for teaching underwent a severe test. I could hardly believe that I would ever be able to step in front of an American class. English is a highly idiomatic language, and I found that mastering it was possible not only through speaking, but, much more important, through writing. I sat down and wrote a lengthy paper. Every sentence had to be rewritten again and again. On each page there were moments of very important discoveries for me. My method helped. What I had thought to be a big hurdle, was conquered when after two years, through the help of the Emergency Committee in Aid of Displaced Foreign Scholars, I became a member of the Art Department of the University of California in Berkeley where I finally taught upper division courses on art connoisseurship. From there I joined the faculty of the Art Department at San Jose State College in California as a professor of art history.

All in all I had six years of teaching experience in America during which I made one of my most enjoyable discoveries, namely, the American student. Although I had to go through hundreds I never had a "reader" for the term papers. I could see the struggle of the student, not too well equipped with what he brought (or rather did not bring) from high school to acquaint himself with a world of bygone cultures. The student's objective in a course is above all to make two or three points. And therein lies the big challenge to the teacher, namely, to create an interest in the subject for its own sake. To have succeeded in this became a source of deep satisfaction time and again.

So there I was, a professor at an American college, living in a lovely California house, with nine fruit trees in the backyard, the idyllic Santa Clara Valley as stamping or rather driving ground, redwood trees and ocean within an hour's reach. A long journey seemed to have come to an end—when out of the truly blue (Californian) sky I was called to The Jewish Theological Seminary of America in New York to serve as Curator and Director of Exhibits at its Museum and to install it in the former mansion of Felix M. Warburg which his widow, Mrs. Frieda Schiff Warburg, had given for that purpose.

I had seen the collections of the Seminary during the two years I had spent in New York doing research work at Columbia University. The valuable objects assembled there, mainly by Professor Alexander Marx, the eminent Librarian of the Seminary, and Dr. Harry G. Friedman, the untiring collector, was a groundwork of which it was hard to prove oneself worthy. New ways had to be found to present these treasures to the public in a museum display which had an entire building at its disposal. The significance of such an undertaking can best be characterized by the words of the famous Jewish historian and collector, Cecil Roth: "It is only during the present generation that serious attention has begun to be paid to Jewish ritual art. Before this, there were indeed a few enthusiastic collectors and eager amateurs. But their enthusiasm was not always in proportion to their discrimination, nor their zeal to their learning, as students of their writings or catalogues periodically discover with a mixture of amusement and alarm. We are now fortunate enough to witness a renaissance in this respect. This is due above all to two causes. One is the work of a handful of scholars trained in the most rigorous European tradition who are devoting themselves to the scientific study of the subject. The other is the emergence of a discriminating few who have developed both a new enthusiasm and a new standard."

In my studies I had always established connections between the arts in general and the artistic needs of the synagogue and the Jewish home. The research which I could do in Bohemia and Moravia on these subjects was particularly enriching. Among the few things I was able to bring to the United States was a sizable collection of slides pertaining to Jewish ritual art.

When this new avenue of endeavor opened to me, I felt at first reluctant to enter into such a venture. The Seminary called me to New York in order to discuss the matter, and midway on my voyage to the East I interrupted the trip and returned to the students, the trees and the mountains of Santa Clara Valley. Months later I met Dr. Louis Finkelstein, at that time President, now Chancellor, of the Seminary, when he came to California in 1946. The discussions with him gave me insight into the structure, the task, and the goal of one of the foremost institutions of Jewish learning in the world today.

To work at the Museum of the Seminary meant, above all, leaving the study hall for quite a while and entering into the task of forming a unit from two things which were entrusted to me, a house with a great name and family tradition, and the collection of the Seminary. Here everything I had experienced and done in my life was to be combined—Judaism, the arts, history, and the interpretation of all these elements. They still needed the catalytic agent which would effect their organic fusion. They had to become a work of art. Destiny had given me that opportunity also in the talents of my wife, who as a creative artist, decorator, and stage designer, fulfilled all the requirements for making a museum display impressive.

Thus, the decision that I had to reach regarding the curatorship of The Jewish Museum in New York was equal to taking stock of my own toils and achievements, together with the help which my wife could give me. Our cooperation resulted in a common work in which it is hard to detect the boundaries of either of our contributions. Without going into details, The Jewish Museum has increased the number of its objects from 2,500 to 5,000, and now has branches in other communities including Chicago, Los Angeles, and Miami Beach, in addition to loan exhibits in leading museums all over the United States. My work as Curator has brought me into close contact with many artists and numerous synagogues in connection with their building activities.

The times of a *vita contemplativa* of which I had once dreamed are far off; my work has become a *vita activa* more than ever before. The discoveries I made in seeing in it a certain plan, are a source of inspiration and satisfaction. Above all, to work in the Jewish field to me means a return. And there is no better return than one by which we feel rewarded and enriched.

V

AN ARTIST PURSUES THE REALITY BENEATH THE APPEARANCE

BY

JOHN FERREN

Confession is a delicate thing. It is delicate because, to be useful to the giver or the receiver, it must be true. It is, I believe, easy to be interesting or amusing in confession while running far from the truth. There is a fascination in hearing anybody talk of his private life, but the fascination quickly takes on another coloring when you begin to talk to yourself. You take on the responsibility and necessity for truth, and when I did so, by request, I found that my "Moments of Discovery" were not allied to dramatic incidents in foxholes, or the like, but were attached to quite small happenings which brought about decisions. The core of any decision is a curious matrix; full, even, of contradictions, and its analysis, after a lapse of time, can be beset by all sorts of dangers from wish fulfilment to just simple lack of memory for what may have been an important detail. However, I find that I have three incidents whose clarity and force have remained with me and have, in my present opinion, guided my life consecutively for the better, the worse, and the better. These have been:

1) A decisive experience of nature with the recognition of a substance or reality beyond the surface aspects of nature.

2) A rejection of this concept, through suffering of a common and relatively superficial nature, and its replacement by another.

3) A reacceptance of the original concept, through the cleansing of personal sorrow and additional insight.

By way of introduction, and so that you may better understand me, I would like to underline the fact that the artist has a closer contact with the physical substance of his craft than does the writer or musician and that it is very difficult, if not impossible, to separate him from his constant concern with the materials of his craft. The brushstroke of the moment must remain for the existence span of the painting. By the same token, the artist has a more perishable art than the writer or musician who communicates through the abstractions of the printed page or printed score. This may explain, somewhat, the tenderness that the artist feels toward the stuff of his art. But deeper than this he knows that his painting is a series of small technical discoveries which first appear, to himself as well as the layman, to be only technical, but which, under the scrutiny and the passage of time, soon change into conceptual and spiritual facts which are really biographies of the personal and inner being of the artist. Thus, if I had my life's work here before you I could illustrate to you, wordlessly, the entire content of my talk. This concept of the lack of division between the technical and the expressive in art directly relates to my present position, both philosophically and spiritually. I do not divide them, and it is no exaggeration for me to say that the discovery of a new pigment could unlock a spiritual corridor or that the understanding of the proper manipulation of the color, yellow, was a spiritual victory for me. My position is that a curved line, a divorce, and an experience of a mystical nature are of the same substance and must be seen in unity to achieve understanding.

I began creative work in my late teens as a sculptor. I had no formal training and I did mainly portrait heads of friends. I first grappled with the surface construction of the head, but once this was fairly mastered, I found that my real concern was shifting toward the inner expression of the individual before me, and I unconsciously began to violate the surface reality that I had just conquered. I emphasized this feature and underplayed that, making my models more or less heroic than they were. My friends soon became too limiting as models and, I may add, somewhat restless. They were either too enthusiastic or too desolated by my renderings. Casting about, I shifted to doing imaginary heads. Here, I felt freer to express what was obviously my necessity of the time, the troubled mental states of my own youth. But this, too, happily, had its term, and more and more the surface aspects of the human form seemed an obstacle to the inner reality which alone interested me. I was, at that time, in an unsatisfied state, without clear purpose, hungry for an intangible, puzzled into near inaction.

For some years previous, I had been subject to experiences which were possibly (I have found no adequate definition) of a mystical nature. None were of great clarity or intensity but they were of sufficient frequency to remain in the memory. These consisted of a sudden sense of identity with certain places in nature, always outside, never in a house. Coupled with a sense of well-being, an "at homeness," would be what I can express only as a sense of identity with the spot in "volume," an awareness of a dimension which encompassed the spot in minute detail but which was certainly not of the customary three dimensions. I am at a loss to rationalize these experiences which still occur. It has been suggested to me that certain conformations in nature accidentally balance at the spot where I am standing and produce a satisfying esthetic response. Also, that the artist tends to develop peripheral vision which can produce a greater volume sense. I am respectful of such interpretations but unimpressed. I prefer to consider these experiences as insights into the nature of reality, or, the reality of nature, if you prefer; insights which are common and available to all but are rarely developed and often rejected in the press of living. For so they have been to me and I prefer to leave the fact of these moments of clarity a mystery and be grateful for them. Creative workers live close to mystery. The creative act is a spontaneous moving. The reasonableness of it becomes apparent later. I am inclined to think that we rush reason in to any pregnant void in our lives too readily. We do so because we fear vagueness. But after all, is the fourth dimension necessarily vague because we do not understand it very well?

On a midafternoon late that summer, I was walking in the hills back of Berkeley, California, with a friend who is now a recognized poet. At one particular spot which is still perfectly clear to me I had the same sensation of identity with place that I have just mentioned, but greatly intensified. I asked my friend if he felt anything peculiar there and he answered, "No." I took a few steps and placed my hand on a tree trunk. I instantaneously felt that every element of the landscape was alive—the light, air, ground, and trees. All were interrelated, living the same life and, this is important to my art, their forms were all interchangeable. The forms of things were only the particular expression of an energy, or substance, which they all shared in common. The "form" was not the "thing." The "thing" was a leaf. Its "form" was an expression of a truth beyond the leaf. All forms were alive and expressive as form first and then as leaves. The intensity of the experience seemed devoted to the penetration of its meaning into my mind.

This was the first decisive incident, written in the only words I can find and as peculiarly unsemantic as all such efforts seem to be. It would be useless to gild or amplify it. It was, in the history of such experiences, a routine one, I am sure, but its effect was to reach over many years. For one, the major perturbations of my youth ceased and I had a clear purpose. As an artist, the concern over the surface aspects of nature stopped and fidelity to them seemed laughable. I had found in this experience of the reality in and behind appearances a coherent philosophy for my art. I concluded that the artist's concern was to reproduce in the spectator the sense of unity which I had felt and knew to be present. I foresaw a directly evocative art rather than a contemplative, intellectual one. The artist was to do this by animating his own materials, his paints and his stone, just as the tree animated its own materials. He was to establish a living interrelationship which would communicate the sense of the ever expanding unity which was ever at hand. For the artist to copy the self-evident beauties of nature was merely praise. His true function was not the praise of nature but the establishing of an identity with nature wherein he functioned with and like nature. Art was the remaking of the inner reality within the restrictions of the artist's medium. Therefore, the medium was, in itself, as full of meanings, interchangeable, varied, and expressive as any particularized growth in nature. The artist must concern himself with his medium as the tree does with its leaf. To use the medium to express the leaf as a "thing" is usurping the tree's function and can please only those who stop at the reality of the leaf.

Thus I established my credo, and although I am somewhat aghast at my youthful temerity in coming to such conclusions without, if you will permit me, benefit of clergy, for I was uneducated at that time in art or anything else, I now, after a lapse of twenty-three years, can subscribe to it word for word with the same abandon and lack of caution while realizing its seriousness.

I had a brief moment of doubt. This sounded like art for art and, in the books I read at the time, this was bad. I reasoned that rejection of the surface reality could not mean art for art, for its avowed function was to open the door to the true reality of nature. This quieted me and I was at peace with my essential purpose.

I changed from sculpture to painting as I became aware of the expressiveness of color. I abandoned with no regret the skill that I had developed in rendering the surface aspects of the world and gave my entire energies to the projection of the "substance" that I had perceived. I was accused of turning my back on nature—the mother of us all. It was true that I had turned my back on the pedestrian view of nature as inherited from the Renaissance via the local calendars, but my personal feeling was that I had walked from the conventional front of nature *into* nature. I could not see how nature could be abandoned anyway, so I was unmoved in my devotion to the "essence" of nature and continued to believe that the language of art could reproduce it. The year was 1930 and I was twenty-five.

Soon after I went to Paris where I married and found spirits congenial to my own. After a few years my work found appreciation and a place in the "abstract" movement which was taking place at that time. All art movements are less closely knit than they appear in the history books, and I later realized that many of the elements in the movement to which I belonged were foreign to my own beliefs and had been arrived at by traditional, intellectual, or didactic means. However, the ends seemed the same and I remained attached to my inner vision of reality and the struggle with the technical means of projecting it. For instance, I became friendly with Picasso and Braque and was often in their studios but I was uninfluenced by their work. They continued to use the surface object and bend it to their purpose. I felt no such compulsion. It was later and in America that I came under their influence. I then shared their world view.

This radical change in view came in a middle crisis which endured

a full ten years. Divorce and first the shadows and then the reality of
World War II were concerned with it. At the time, 1937 and 1938,
Paris, the world, and my personal life were in a state of ferment. I am
still unable to trace all of the many things that must have influenced
me. I had no interest in politics. I read mainly the classics. My friends
were many and busy with the business of living and art. Certainly the
about face which I soon undertook did not stem from any practical,
careerwise situation. I was doing well in my painting itself and sales
and appreciation were going apace. However, the relatively minor
tragedy of divorce seemed to be the trigger which unlatched a full
revolt against my own concepts of what were the purpose and content of art.

One incident of this time remains in my mind and, regardless of
its slightness, appears to have been the catalytic agent which confirmed
my reversal of position. I was walking down a Paris street suffering
from the pain, disillusion, self-doubts, regrets, and desires of marital
separation. A woman was coming toward me, walking quickly, ab-
sorbed in her own happy thoughts. She was neither pretty nor not
pretty. I remember no detail. She was simply a woman, a person, a
symbol. She was quietly happy and I was very unhappy. Suddenly, I
saw us both as human beings, members of the same species, and I
was flooded with a wave of pity. Pity for her, pity for me and pity
for everybody. Because she was human she was now happy but she
would be unhappy. I became acutely aware of the human state and I
concluded that man's only concern should be with the inevitable un-
happiness of man. In the moment before she passed I abandoned my
concern with what I have called the "substance" of nature. That was
something too near the angels and too far from the misery of man.
I returned home and wrote in my sketchbook, "Art is the communication of man to man and the only thing that man can or should
understand is the misery and hope of man." I was then thirty-three
years old, but still, obviously, too little adult to suspect this sublimation
of the personal into the universal or to realize that I was also suffering
from a lack of faith. I stopped painting in the abstract and did a series
of tragic heads. Picasso approved and said that they were premonitions
of war. Premonitions or not, Munich came and went. I returned to

America. War broke out and the misery of the world confirmed to me my change of view. I remarried and spent three years reverting to the reconquest of the surface aspects of nature. I painted apples on a plate, made endless drawings of the human figure, and vainly tried to acquire the vocabulary that would clarify man to man. In a sense, I re-enacted the history of the development of Occidental painting. I went to my own art school. But, while feeling morally and intellectually justified, I was not content. No light penetrated and I did not exhibit. I went to war myself in a state of puzzled discouragement.

A daughter was born after my departure and after three years overseas I returned to another divorce and the added disorientation of the veteran. I picked up painting where I had stopped before the war and continued redoing the history of contemporary painting. I worked up to Picasso and Braque, exhibited, and was hailed by the critics as a new and more "human" Ferren. I continued, still discontent, and my work evolved in appearance to something approaching what I had been doing ten to twelve years before. In effect, I had arrived intellectually at a form of painting which I had formerly perceived intuitively. I had apparently rounded out a circle to arrive where I had already been, which is a pretty discouraging fact. Ten years seemed to have been lost. My "humanist" decision had not been tenable. My own studies had evolved beyond it. In one sense, I had won a hard fought intellectual battle. I had thoroughly plowed the other side of the fence, planted it, and found the fruit tasteless. I was now back on my own side. The view was familiar but the spontaneous heart, the conviction of the inner source, was lacking. I was on a high level impasse. I was reminded of it while driving the long and imperceptible rise before the Great Divide in Wyoming which, after hours of travel, suddenly lifts itself to a summit and the same landscape that was flatness before becomes splendor all around. I broke over the summit through tragedy.

My daughter, aged 7, was killed in an accident and I was informed of it while on vacation in California. In that real and bottomless sorrow which is loss of your own, I rolled in the grass like a sick animal. When, how much later I do not know, I opened my eyes—nature was before me much as I had seen it twenty years before in the Berkeley hills, and I was comforted. My first conscious thought was: "She cannot see this," and a new wave of sorrow swept the brief insight away.

But, with the subsiding of sorrow came an upsurge of interest in my old "essence" of nature. I remembered the brief moment in the middle of grief and its reality seemed valid and permanent. It consoled where no consolidation seemed possible. Almost imperceptibly, I realized that I was over the hump. The circle had not closed. I now had emotional and spiritual justification for return to the faith of my boyhood. I was permitted to be alive and for my original purpose. Once again, I saw the true "usefulness" of the artist to be in his penetration into the sources of his being and in the communication of the reality which lies beyond appearances. He does not emulate God by copying His works nor in producing symbols which lead the mind to contemplation. He proves Him on man's level by showing in his work the indissoluble unity of matter, substance, and spirit. This concept could be new and reflect a new world image, or, more probably, it is the essence of a past which we have lost. It is certainly not the "mystical or spiritual" painting of the Annie Besant, self-styled, handwriting of God school, and any tieup with ideologies of that sort can do incalculable harm, for they tend to negate matter, and painting is first matter. It describes matter, if not always appearances. It is not by neglecting matter but by imbuing it with life that we make apparent the spirit. I do not believe that this concept is particular to me. I see it at the core of contemporary art and it is the key to its manufacture by the artist and to its understanding by the layman.

So, personally, I no longer have any quarrel with appearance or with abstraction. The truth is fleshier than abstraction and the skin of appearances is true but is only a footnote to a greater rhythm. Both are, at bottom, intellectual conceptions.

Of the other reality of what I conceived to be "humanism" and the contact with man through appearances, I now believe that man does not profit from the sympathy or pity which come by showing him as he is trapped in his humanity. Only one thing breaks his loneliness— the infiltration of matter by the spirit. The quest for this seems to me to be the only valid one for every man beyond his subsistence, and the only authentic one for the artist, who is traditionally careless of his subsistence. It is the meaning of art and the true reason for every man going to art. Any willed program, willed from the inside or the outside, which substitutes another purpose, no matter how noble sounding, is violating the unity of matter and spirit, and such violations are destructive of the maker and the receiver. Violation is inevitable if matter, substance, or spirit are treated separately or pitted one against the other.

I arrived at this conviction through the incidents just related. Undramatic as they are, it is they that have "fired my imagination"—and it remains fired.

VI

I ENLIST IN THE CAUSE OF JUSTICE

BY

IRVING BEN COOPER

My childhood was an ugly one. I was always worried and frightened. There were six of us, six children, and I felt the obligation, as keenly as did my parents, that the rent must be paid on the first of the month. It was a constant issue, as was the grocery bill. Whether or not this boy's shoes could be repaired that month, and could he now take the cardboard out of the shoe—it was that sort of thing. Then, too, a lack of understanding between the parents—the bickering, bickering. It was walking to school the crooked way to avoid being called "sheeny" and the recipient of blows from all and sundry. Constantly absent was the smile. Of all the teachers I ever had, the few I fondly remember were those who smiled at me.

Picking up the coal that fell from the railroad cars to the tracks—picking up that coal with fingers frozen so that I had to cup my hands in order to hold it, and bring it home to feed the pot-bellied stove, the only source of physical warmth—was not the heartache. The heartache was the absence of someone to talk to and confide in, someone who would understand. And all around me there was evidence of hurts, wounds, injustices that I saw affect not only the lives of the members of my family but many families in the same house and on the same street and in the same neighborhood.

From my mother who had that enormous washboard wash on Monday and the floor scrubbing, especially in preparation for the Sabbath, I caught the spirit of religion—nothing of a formal character. And something else influenced me, and this is a confession: whether you put them in the category of literature or not, I just simply loved those Horatio Alger books. I avidly read the life stories of boys whose childhood was as raw and naked as my own. The copybook maxims were to me an inspiration.

The determination to progress and get out of that environment brought about the unswerving determination to attend college. For seven years, like many others—I am just telling my story and it is not unique—I worked for everything from shoelaces to tuition. There was not a penny from any outside source.

I was not much of a student. How can you be working ten hours a day at some job, seven days a week, weighing 105, 106 pounds, never going to a game, never having much of a chance of buying anything besides bare necessities. And I found that I moved to wherever there was a job and so attended four different institutions of learning.

When I came to be admitted to the Bar in New York City, and the questionnaire put me on notice that I would have to swear to the contents of that application, I was distinctly ordered to "List each and every job you ever held." I remember the number—sixty-three— from washing dishes to teaching; from janitoring to selling on the road. And I had to furnish satisfactory proof, and such was the price of truthfulness that by the time I got around to getting all that proof, I was delayed admission to the Bar by six months.

Of course all of this took its toll physically, as well as emotionally. But these experiences of mine, in order to survive, to get ahead, took a certain kind of courage, the kind of courage about which I had read so much and with deep impression. And so when I committed "Invictus" to heart, I felt the tremendous force of its concluding lines:

> I am the master of my fate;
> I am the captain of my soul.

On rare occasions, thank God, I met those whose behavior I considered exemplary. It seemed always to come from those with friendly eyes and a face aglow with goodwill. These people seemed to have hearts sensitive to the sighs, the wails, the laments of men and women stricken, bereaved, and broken. Their labors of love, I detected, were not sporadic or occasional, but constant and habitual.

Yet there were times when my spirit sagged and the goal seemed barred. It was then that I refused to believe that those were hollow lines that I had memorized:

Say not the struggle naught availeth, the labor and the wounds are
   vain, . . .
In front, the sun climbs slow, how slowly,
But westward, look, the land is bright.

Then, too, those early experiences brought me close to the simple people and simple things—the things with which men and women work. I found ordinary life warm, and was pained with those who spurned it, for men, as the poet has said, "Cease to build beautiful churches when they have lost happiness in building shops."

At the same time, these experiences of mine taught me to hate cruelty and insincerity and vulgarity, and to despise all those who climb on the shoulders of their fellowmen.

After I was admitted to the Bar, I took a position as clerk in a good law office, and then something happened to me which is the kernel of the subject of this chapter.

I was given the ordinary assignments that a clerk receives at the hands of his employer. I certainly was not writing the briefs; I was running down to the County Clerk's office and filing papers. But there came a day—I was there about a year and a half—when my chance arrived. I was going to go to a court and represent my law firm. The firm counted among its clients wealthy men in the real estate field, and so on this particular case, I represented a landlord who was the firm's client. The question was: Did the tenant abuse his tenancy in such a manner as to entitle the landlord to an order of eviction?

I prepared the case with everything in me. This was what I had waited for. This was what all that life was about. I arrived in the Bronx from Brooklyn—and we then lived in an eighteen dollar a month railroad flat—on the dot of nine. Stupid—but I was there! Irving Ben Cooper was the only one in the room. The courtroom door happened to be open, undoubtedly through the carelessness of a civil servant, and I sat there. About a quarter of ten the clerk came in, along with a few other persons. I sat toward the front row, ready, anxious—too anxious, possibly—and then around ten o'clock the name of the case in which I was interested was called by the clerk. The judge, of course, had not yet arrived. I got up quickly and the clerk said, "He wants to talk to you," and he pointed to a man I never saw before. The man said, "I am the lawyer for the tenant. I'm not waiting around. You're a damn fool for hanging around here. Get on back to your office. It's all fixed!"

I could hardly catch my breath when the fellow was gone. Around eleven o'clock His Honor got on the bench, and about ten after eleven, this case, this all important cause célèbre was called. Here, here was my chance. I jumped up and ran so quickly—I can remember it vividly —I almost ran into the bench itself. "Ready, Your Honor!" "You for the landlord?" "Yes, Your Honor." "Judgment for the tenant." "But, Your Honor I wish to present my proof here, my evidence." The judge rose, wrapped his gown around him, pointed his finger at me and said with disdain, "You are undoubtedly a new lawyer, huh? In my court all the judgments go to the tenants. They elected me and they get my judgments."

I protested. The next case was called. I will spend no more than a half moment to tell you that every molecule in my body revolted. I was outraged. I saw impartial justice spat upon. With all the inequities I had observed in the business field, I had always felt that in the legal arena I could champion my cause if only I applied courage and devotion. I went back and reported this to my superior, a kindly man, and he said, "That's going on all the time." "But can't we appeal? I'll work. I'll work Sundays and nights. I'll put all my time in. Please, can't we go ahead with this?" "It doesn't pay. It doesn't pay." He added, "We have just got to devote our attention to our clients, and I know that this is a terrible experience, but I am fully aware that it is constant."

Then I began to inquire intensively. This outrage was more than just a case. My employer was sympathetic, understanding. He knew I had tried. *It was what that man was doing in the name of justice that unnerved me, that tormented me.* I learned that my abhorrent court experience was but an insignificant part of the total evidence supporting the proposition that ofttimes there just simply was no justice.

What was to become of my firm belief that every lawyer was a public servant; that he becomes an officer of the courts as soon as he is admitted, a guardian of the general good as soon as he has taken his oath? Then it was not true that the judge and the lawyers were "sleepless sentinels on the ramparts of justice, ever ready to sound the alarm when an enemy appears!"

I left that firm and went into private practice where at first I was my own clerk, stenographer, telephone operator, and advocate-at-law. And while the practice was building, slowly, there came an opportunity. The Association of the Bar of New York City and other associations of lawyers asked for volunteers to help clean out of the profession those who were bringing disgrace to it by downright thievery, fraudulent releases, fake medical certificates, phony cases, and causes of action. As I saw it, they were like the lawyer who told me the case was "all fixed." I volunteered and threw body, heart, and soul into the work, not knowing of food or sleep. Hundreds of witnesses day after day paraded before me, and I wrung them white of the true facts—facts that would stand up against all attack.

The evidence showed that these lawyers—and I am grateful to be able to say that they constituted a very small percentage of the total—had grown fat; how they hobnobbed with judges! Their influence was unbearable; they pushed aside the struggling little fellow at the Bar and set up their highpowered operations which completely overwhelmed their brethren at the Bar. They contributed nothing to the advancement of legal precepts or improvement of standards at the Bar or in the courts. Their contacts with politicians were powerful and defiant. Thus the political-judicial-attorney combination was extremely hard to open.

Clients, witnesses, all and sundry concerned with the supposed due administration of justice participated in perjury and subornation of perjury. All were led to believe that foul play was the order of the day. How unfair, unprincipled, corrosive! What irreparable damage!

So strong and determined were the hands of the investigation that the searing light of truth exposed the corrupt practices, dragged the offenders before the bar of justice where their misdeeds were recounted, followed by orders of disbarment entered of record as well as the imposition of jail sentences. Thereafter court rules were promulgated which tightened the loopholes and put all on notice that unworthy practitioners at the bar would be dealt with summarily. And so personal conduct at the bar—much more circumspect and of high order—prevailed for a long time.

And who were the handful of men who headed that inquiry? They were men who were angry in the cause of decency; men with whom a principle is not a thing you talk about, but a thing you *do* something about; men who realize that it is difficult to fight for principles but much more difficult to live by them. Yes, they were men angry in their conviction; men unable to compromise with injustice; men placed among us as standards against which we can measure our own integrity. Men who serve *with* honor and not *for* honor. Their sense of dedication spurred me on.

While engaged in private practice again, I received a call from Judge Samuel Seabury. Would I be interested in helping to clean out the Magistrates Courts? He pointed out that in that busy tribunal, practices were being engaged in every day which amounted to corrupt arrangements; that innocent people were the victims of false and disgraceful charges; that defendants were—to use the vernacular —"kicked around," and that the little man was denied justice and so there was no justice.

I met this fearless champion of decency and saw that out of a world full of human limitations a man rises; out of all the half-truths, the comfortable rationalizations, the turning away of the eye from the galling facts of life; out of so much misery a man rises and says, "I go this way and not there. I am this, and not that. I have no price but only value." Indeed, I saw that for those who build their safety in things, and things alone, there is no greater threat, no more incomprehensible danger than such a man—a man in pursuit of truth.

I enlisted in the cause. The charges were proven: corruption had been running riot. The Court was purged and due process of law came into its own again.

Once more I returned to practice. Then again a call from Judge Seabury to associate myself with him in the inquiry into all the governmental departments of the city. Vice prevailed and impious men held sway. At every turn the evidence revealed the low level of iniquity to which men in power—in and out of public office—had sunk. While the public slept, they plundered all and sundry and the sky was the limit. The voting public, indifferent to the obligations of citizenship, had unwittingly aided and abetted the perpetrators.

In time the force of these disclosures compelled vigorous action and LaGuardia went to City Hall. No history of this country dealing with this first half-century can be accurately written without devoting a significant chapter to the outstanding contribution to the commonweal by those two stalwarts, LaGuardia and Seabury.

Other posts furnished opportunity for additional public service. Not all the forces of evil were beaten off, but from it all came that deep inner satisfaction of a job well done. Evidence abounds in the form of a thousand worthwhile examples to prove that we labored not in vain.

One instance I like to contemplate concerned the Old Age Home on Welfare Island to which the aged and the homeless and the friendless were committed; whose inmates scrubbed floors and performed similar tasks for a pittance which they saved meticulously over the years with the comforting knowledge that some day there would be enough to warrant their release from institutional care and return to the city where they could live out their remaining years in quiet and independence. And the proof which I gathered further disclosed that these precious savings were cunningly appropriated by an avaricious superintendent. That was the same institution, you remember, where medical facilities were actually unknown; an old seahand performed operations with a penknife.

The scandal quickly demolished those buildings. Now there stands the Goldwater Memorial Hospital, a model institution of its kind. Some of the leading skin specialists have concentrated their studies there, and medicine and humanity, in turn, have been the beneficiaries.

And yet, from it all there is still much that distresses me. I see all too many driven by the feverish desire to obtain financial and social success at any and all costs. Many are in high places. That the cost includes the washing away of one's peculiar and individual propensities and talents, which in themselves may be healthy and productive, matters not. They certainly cannot be relied upon to concern themselves with communal well-being.

And there are many, including those in high places and others who should know better, who minimize outrageous behavior. I am not talking about a mooted question on ethics—I am talking about laws that are on the books and pronounced crimes; not insignificant offences but crimes that go to the very moral behavior of the individual.

How many minimize that kind of behavior! "Why should I stick my neck out?" is what they want to know. "Why should I speak out?" And from still others there is the constant, "What's in it for me?" Or, "What's your angle?" And, of course, you constantly get the familiar, "You've got to get along!"

What is particularly aggravating is the growing conviction on the part of all kinds of people that whatever we hope for and whatever we do are irrelevant; that our individual efforts really make no difference in stemming the sweep of world forces. To me this mood of resignation is but a desire to escape from the problems of freedom, a fear of growing up and maturely accepting one's responsibilities. They have lost faith—if they ever had any—in the efficacy of effort. Because they are suffering they make others suffer; tormented by fear, they make others afraid.

Then, too, I find tolerance misapplied. So many use it as an easy means to look the other way. Dr. Robert J. McCracken called their bluff when he said, "In nine cases out of ten what goes by the name of tolerance is really apathy. . . . It is less than a virtue if it weakens the critical faculty or weakens the instinct for what is just and right." [1]

---

[1] An excerpt from Doctor McCracken's sermon, "Tolerance Is Not Enough," quoted in *The New York Times,* Monday, April 28, 1952.

What is particularly depressing to me is that so much courage is kept under wraps for such long periods of time. That is always the signal for the contemptuous rascals, who somehow always succeed in enticing the good and the bad, the high and the lowly, to stay on their side and "go to town." Milton knew this when he wrote, "Good and evil grow up together almost inseparably," they grow fat and oppressive. Unseating all of them is impossible; doing it to a few is accomplished only at overwhelming costs. What price timidity!

And then, there is lipservice religion—religion without spadework. I call upon Dr. McCracken again:

Too many people think that religion is something apart from life in the everyday world. They need to be shown that they are wrong by people who take their religion with them right into the thick of the world and put it to work there. By and large, we Christians are not making anything like an adequate attempt to influence the pattern of society. We are not involving ourselves deeply enough in public affairs—the education of the young, the care of the sick and the old, the prevention of delinquency and crime, the undergirding of the community by voluntary social service. We tend, most of us, to concentrate on a private piety which is at little pains to relate itself to civic situations. To keep Christianity hoarded and locked up inside our churches often means that in the end it is not even there.[2]

I have the honor to head a court where for many years I sat as an associate trial justice. Here I find as great a challenge as any that dared me to enter the open lists to win or lose. What do you do with the youthful first offender with good moral potential? Is it sufficient to weigh the facts, apply the law, and pronounce judgment? Should we not concern ourselves with his rehabilitation?

After all, while endless debates go on concerning the correct blueprint for Utopia, we must concern ourselves with the tremendous force of simple truths: we realize that poverty of mind and spirit is as awful as poverty of the body; that in indifference to misery and helplessness lies disaster. We know that in a fuller, richer, real democracy, everyone counts; we know the significance of imbuing each person with a sense of belonging.

[2] An excerpt from the sermon, "Setting Our Goals for 1953," quoted in *The New York Times*, January 5, 1953.

So we are determined to help teach these young people to under-stand the minds of others, to weigh *their* interests alongside their own without bias of any kind; pointing out that it is "not wisdom to be only wise," as Santayana put it; urge them to get rid of false estimates and set up the higher ideals; and convince them that in our social order the ladder of opportunity is not so high above the ground that you must have a ladder of influence to reach the lowest rung.

From the constant heartache of my boyhood to this very mo-ment, I have witnessed a veritable panorama of human nature—be-hind the scenes, never before unburdened, naked. To absorb the full significance of it all and still carry on, what real comfort and strength there is in a simple religion empty of all bigotry but full of trust and hope and love! And add to it a boundless courage to cry out against injustice in any form.

What I have been trying to say was said much better about 125 years ago in the London *Times:*

The greatest tyranny has the smallest beginnings. From precedents over-looked, from remonstrances despised, from grievances treated with ridi-cule, from powerless men oppressed with impunity, and overbearing men tolerated with complacence, springs the tyrannical usage which genera-tions of wise and good men may hereafter perceive and lament and resist in vain.

At present, common minds no more see a crushing tyranny in a trivial unfairness or a ludicrous indignity, than the eye uninformed by reason can discern the oak in the acorn or the utter desolation of winter in the first autumnal fall.

Hence the necessity of denouncing with unwearied and even trouble-some perseverance a single act of oppression. Let it alone and it stands on record. The country has allowed it, and when it is at last provoked to a late indignation it finds itself gagged with the record of its own ill-compulsion.

VII

DISCOVERY IS THE CUTTING EDGE OF LEARNING

BY

KARL W. DEUTSCH

You have given me the task, as to all speakers in this series, to discuss something called, "Moments of Personal Discovery." At once I find myself constrained to ask, "What is meant by the word, 'discovery'? What is it that anyone of us discovers, or more particularly, what is it that we discover in social science?"

To answer these questions, I should like to suggest that there are about five different stages or processes interwoven in the making of discoveries.

The first of these is the discovery of *problem areas*. It is the sum of experiences somewhere along the path of your life, telling you that this or that broad area is important, that it deserves attention, and that it should have something done about it by such people as yourselves.

The second is the discovery of *specific problems;* and it may take many years between the discovery of a problem area and the discovery, or emergence, or formulation, of a specific problem in sharp terms.

The third set of discoveries, going on during the same years of our lives, is the discovery of *resources*. Sometimes we discover problems long before we discover any resources for dealing with them. Sometimes, again, we discover resources before we discover the problems. This is true in the history of science. The Greek mathematicians, Archimedes and Apollonius, discovered techniques of mathematics which turned out later to be applicable to problems of Renaissance technology, but these mathematical resources were discovered 1700 years before the problems. Similarly, in everyday life we may sometimes find a lock, but still lack the key to open it. Sometimes again we may find a bunch of keys, and we may have to look for the locks which they will fit.

The fourth set of discoveries is the discovery of relations between particular locks and particular keys. This is the discovery of *relevant connections*. It consists in finding that this particular set of facts, this type of attack, this particular tool in the arsenal of science, will be suitable or meaningful for dealing with this particular kind of problem.

Only finally, after you have discovered your problem area, and your battery of resources, and your particular problem, and your particular relations of relevance, somewhere along this line—but late along this line—will you make your first discoveries of *solutions*.

All this does not necessarily mean that you need to know all the time that you are going through this routine. You need not be aware of the fact that you are working your way along this assembly line of ideas. It is perfectly possible that you "know," first of all, that you have a solution. You then ask yourself, "How did it happen that I became interested in this problem?"—and you may find that ten years earlier there was an experience that put this problem into your mind. "Where," you then ask, "did I acquire the techniques for solving it?" —and you may find that three years ago you found some of the techniques which you are now using. You may have put all this somewhere in your memory without paying any particular attention to it at that time. We remember more things, it seems to me, than we are aware of, or than we can consciously recall. Only when all these things get together, only then do we become aware of a seemingly readymade solution; and then, by asking questions of ourselves, we may find out how the parts of this solution invisibly became assembled, perhaps some years before, unnoticed, in our minds.

I have spoken of solutions, and I should like to divide these solutions into two broad groups:

The first of these are the so-called "objective" or "theoretical" solutions. Here a problem is stated in general terms. Is there a solution for it? Is there, that is to say, a *pattern of resources* that should make it possible to get a certain action performed, or to wipe out a particular obstacle, to ameliorate a certain disorder, a certain case of injustice, or suffering? For an example of such an objective solution, think of being caught in a traffic jam. As your car is standing there, wedged in behind the others, you may suddenly realize that there is an objective way of looking at this situation. Is there a way in which this traffic could flow freely? What is the best traffic pattern to solve the long run problem of traffic at this intersection?

Then there is the second type, the "acceptable" or "practical" solution. Here you are given, perhaps, the present driving habits of your contemporaries; the present state of the city budget; the present width of the houses and sidewalks, and the unwillingness of the corner owner to sell, in order to widen the street. Given these data, what is the solution most likely to be accepted here and now? That is the "practical" way of finding a solution at the moment.

I suspect that, on the whole, executive ability and political leadership are found in those people who excel in finding the short range solutions; and that leadership in fundamental science, and perhaps prophetic leadership in either ethics or religion, are shown by people who can see the long range fundamental solutions which still may seem unimaginable or unacceptable to many of their contemporaries.

The people with the fundamental solutions, therefore, have a very good chance of getting into trouble with their neighbors who may resent their new ideas. On the other hand, these people with the fundamental solutions have a very good chance of getting their contemporaries into trouble, if they try to put their fundamental solutions into effect immediately, without paying much attention to the details of practicality, and the felt needs of people here and now.

In any case, whether you are more interested in fundamental ideas, or in ideas that are immediately practical, you will find in the story of your own life a collection of overlapping sequences of discoveries. We discover solutions for some long pursued problems at the same stage in our lives as we discover seemingly relevant facts in regard to other problems which we cannot as yet solve. We discover resources that seem significant to us in relation to the whole ensemble of problems which hold, or yet may come to hold, our interest; and we discover problems and problem areas for which we may not as yet have either any pertinent resources, or even any explicit formulation.

Our minds, I believe, work with just such areas and classes of problems; with arsenals and batteries of resources; they work with specific connections of relevance just discovered or constructed. They work with constructs of our thoughts thrown forward like bridges or scaffoldings over a precipice of the unknown, or like stormladders over the moats of ignorance. Yet at the same time our minds work with solutions that seem to come to us in the quieter moments of all this activity, when we disengage, as it were, our attention from pressing the search for just such answers.

I think we can find examples for all this in the lives of many scientists; and perhaps the inherent multiplicity of our discoveries may help to explain the empirical fact that so many creative scientists do not remain confined to the study of a single field or to the making of a single contribution.

Obviously, the account I have just given cannot pretend to be an objective description. At best, it is a vague statement shot through with autobiographical data. Having perceived this, you now may well ask me to be specific. What have been my own moments of discovery, and what, if anything, can I claim to have discovered in them?

The only answers I can offer will be in terms of four or five groups of experiences.

The first is the discovery of problem areas. To the best of my knowledge, certain problem areas have interested me since childhood. I discovered far back in childhood something of the change and separation that war meant. One of the first experiences I can remember is the experience of my father coming home, an unknown man in uniform with a mustache, on leave from the army in World War I.

The second experience I remember is a city draped in black at the death of an Austrian emperor, and I experienced the sharp clash between that which is normal and that which seems to be disturbing. The fact has remained that the first thing I remember about an emperor is that he dies. The impression that power is perishable thus came early.

The third memory I have of public affairs is the flag draped city of Prague and the wild enthusiasm of the crowds at the time of the end of World War I, on October 28, 1918, and their feeling of liberation. There was peace, and the empire was replaced by a republic. I remembered that a people can feel released, can feel liberated. It sounds a strange thing to remember in this world of today when so many countries are back under one or another form of oppression; but the experiences of liberation and not of oppression stuck in my mind.

I remember the invisible effects of war when I remember the horror —it is not too strong a word—on the face of my father when he saw a long bladed hunting knife; it reminded him of the trench knives handed out in the army.

I remember my mother's campaign, standing for parliament, and the look on the faces of simple people who elected her, when some of their hopes, fears, and aspirations were given expression; when their dreams were put into words; and when some action for a better life was started.

Such actions were in fact taken. I remember a period of about ten years, from 1919 to 1929, when housing went up, when schools were built, when something real was done for health, for education, for liberty, for decency, for making life better in some concrete way.

All those experiences, then, gave me one broad problem area in which I would remain receptive to discoveries.

Another group of experiences cast a different light on this same area. While attending Latin school, I also became first an apprentice, and then a journeyman in a skilled trade. I became an optician in my afternoons, in addition to studying science, languages, and literature in the mornings. Soon I discovered that the man next to me in the workshop had the same abilities as I had, but that he had not had the chance to get the education I was getting. Somehow I gained from this the impression that having any kind of education is a social privilege that implies a social responsibility; that knowledge, acquired in a world where not many people can acquire knowledge, should be used in the service of other people. At the same time I gained a sense of workmanship. I discovered that you cannot argue with tools. You cannot argue with the material out of which you are trying to shape some piece of goods. Some part of a machine or some optical device must be satisfied on its own terms and by its own standards. I learned that there must be technical competence or workmanship, and that where this workmanship is lacking, fluency with words will not replace the actual work that has not been done.

Out of all this, there came an awareness of a double problem area. Something is owed to mankind by anybody with an education. It is their duty to try to help people who need help. This help, however, can only be given in a workmanlike manner. The problem of bettering even slightly the condition of the people of the world, is a large sized one. It is a major material task to be performed, and it is not possible to be entirely vague about it. There is a technical, workmanlike job to be done about it.

Perhaps these experiences added up to the notions of responsibility and reform, and the notions of knowledge and action, which should in some way be at least related to each other.

Superimposed upon this growing area of awareness and concern was the steady impact throughout the education of my generation, made by such people as T. G. Masaryk; and particularly the impact of his notion that democracy was based on our attitude toward the worth of each individual human being.

When I later came to study in England, I took part in a two weeks walking tour over the Scottish Highlands with a group of English and Scottish students. I had been on such trips before, in Germany and elsewhere. But when you went on a hike as a Central European, you had a skipper, or you elected a skipper—a leader who told you what to do. But with these people, when we went over the Scottish Highlands, we had cooked our meals and swept our rooms, and nobody had ever told anybody what to do. Yet, everything got done all the time. People had learned, the English and Scots student had learned, how to carry on teamwork in a voluntary manner. They were sensitive enough to know when something was not getting done; and if so, they went and did it.

It was possible, I realized, to have a high degree of precision and efficiency, together with a very high level of freedom, provided that people were attentive, thoughtful, and sensitive enough to make the constant effort which was needed for it. This manner of living could replace the cruder method of having everything commanded by a leader, or ordered by some rigid schedule or plan.

In some ways, this experience led me to think for the next twenty years or so about the problem of freedom. How does freedom work? What does freedom require? How can people direct their own lives so that they can work with others without denying their own autonomy?

Of course, you can say, all this is a very vague and general attitude. Even so, let me add one more impression here, namely, that the search for the good life, for human values to be realized in a human context, seems to me in some way bound up with a notion as to where mankind fits into a context that is greater than mankind. In other words, the problem of religion, "What are man's obligations in a world that is greater than himself?" and the problem of ethics, "What are man's obligations to other men?" have seemed to me, from as far back as I can remember, part and parcel of the same thing.

This was a handful of problems, as you can readily see, and the chances of doing anything about any of them seemed rather doubtful.

However, the problems became worse in the 1930's, and I became aware of specific details among them. There was the fact that my parents used one language—German—at home but another elsewhere. I spoke German or Czech with my school friends, but in the street, at times, it was not safe to speak German. In other cities, it might have been safe to speak them both, but the fact that the speech of parents to their children should be affected by national conflicts among their neighbors was something that I remembered for a long time. I remember the gradual worsening of these nationalistic clashes and conflicts. I visited Germany in 1930; I was there during the

electoral campaign in which the Nazi Party rose from the insignificant
sect it had been to the largest political party in the country. I saw, in
the following years, and remember to this day, the faces of the Nazi
students walking through Prague with the disdainful expression on
their faces of a master race among their supposed inferiors.

I remember a meeting in which a Czech student was killed a row
of seats away from me, by Czech Fascists who were trying to introduce the Nazi creed, complete with stiff arm greeting, into the Czech
community. The attempt of this political movement failed; by and
large, the Czech students stayed solidly democratic; but I noticed at
that time that the behavior pattern of violence and killing was not in
any way limited to any one nation, any one language group, or even
any one religion. I discovered that, regardless of whatever particular
theory, religion, or politics professed, the temptation to use the short-
cuts of violence and tyranny seemed ever present.

Anybody who has grown up in the 1930's has had colleagues who
became Communists. He may remember their quick shifts from
ruthlessness to bitter disillusionment. He may remember the spectacle
of brilliant minds fettered by shackles which were self-imposed;
which were of their own seeking and making.

What was going on? What forced people to throw away self-
determination, autonomy, freedom, and responsibility for themselves?
These were more specific problems which emerged within the broader
problem area.

Where did some of the intellectual resources for working on these
problems come from? Some of them I can sketch here: a European
Latin school, where ancient Rome becomes as vivid as yesterday's
headlines. It is the kind of thing that we cannot present easily in an
American institution of education. In Europe some of the cobblestones
are a thousand years old, and the past lives for you with a reality
which is hard to come by otherwise.

I remember the contact I had with science and workmanship later
on at Northampton Engineering College in the University of London, where the emphasis was on quantitative, structural, and partly
mathematical thinking. Can you measure it? Can you test it? Can
you build it, rebuild it, and make a replica of it? Can you put qualita-

tive knowledge together with quantitative and structural knowledge, so that it can be taken apart and put together again?

There were other resources which came—an interest in poetry, as expressed in a definition by W. H. Auden. If you read a poem, you sometimes say, "I have always felt like this, but I couldn't put it into words, and now I can." This, says Auden, is good poetry. But sometimes, says Auden, you read a poem and say, "I never felt like this, and now I know what it is like to feel like this." That, says Auden, is great poetry. Poetry, in this sense, to my mind has a bearing on the kind of work you do in science. There is something in common between the discovery of a true proposition in natural science; a correct interpretation in social science; an elegant proof in mathematics; a happy formulation in poetry; and a significant color in a painting. In all these, there are certain properties of the problem to be met, an economy of resources to be used, and a power or validity required of the solution to be created or selected.

Possibly one of the most important resources, in addition to the technical training in natural or social science, have been the experiences coming from the contact with religion. The strongest religious influence I can remember is that of Protestantism. I remember the statue put up in Prague for John Hus, the founder of the Czech Protestants, who was burned for his faith in 1415. I later came to the city of Constance, on Lake Constance, where the stones and the houses told the story of past religious intolerance, and the long way toward mutual religious tolerance that had to be traveled. I remember how this impression was reinforced later on by the discovery of the reality and the depth of the Protestant tradition in England and the United States. One of the strongest impressions I received was in Wallingford, Connecticut, in the Episcopal Communion Services in the Choate Chapel.

Though my strongest impressions were Protestant, I grew up in a Catholic part of Europe; that is to say, I grew up in a world of Europeans of the Catholic faith and Catholic thought; many of my memories were shaped by the whole Catholic culture of the people, and by the testimony of their cathedrals.

I remember also one experience I had that did more than anything else to fix in my mind an appreciation of the resources, character, and depth of the Jewish tradition. It was in a small and lonely village on the border of French and Spanish Morocco, on a scorching hot day in August, 1933. To this day the sight of the small Arab boys playing in the dust around the village fountain stays in my memory. There was not a single Jewish child to be seen in the streets. But then we heard a singsong sound, and as we followed it, we came into a little side alley, and there was a door which was open, and in there was a room with about thirty children, squatting on the floor, swaying from side to side, and chanting the letters of the Hebrew alphabet; and we realized that for two thousand years in places like El Ksar el Kebir, on the edge of the African desert, literacy had been preserved in the most unlikely surroundings. There and then I realized the tremendous effort that had been made to keep alive the tradition of thinking and reading under such conditions.

The next great group of resources was the impact of American social science; the discovery that American economics was far ahead of the economics of most European universities; the discovery that there were both qualitative and quantitative methods available in American political science and sociology; that there was an attitude of intelligent inquiry, of tolerance and cheerful skepticism. There followed the discovery of the tremendous work done at a place like Massachusetts Institute of Technology; the discovery of their machines which can do things very similar to human thinking; the discovery that there are human teams who can accomplish more than an individual can. There came the discovery of teamwork in research and group research, which was then reinforced by the experience of doing this kind of work for the government in the Office of Strategic Services and the State Department. I was responsible for leading such research teams for two years, and I found out how much can be done in the solving of problems that would be beyond the abilities of one man alone.

Out of this came certain propositions about relevance. From those problems and those resources inferences could be drawn. Thus what the economists had discovered about the forces of an impersonal labor market might have some direct application to the importance of language in affecting everybody's work. You could assume that, as people had to compete with each other for jobs in an insecure society, they might tend to fall back on language and national culture in order to acquire for themselves and their services the equivalent of the position of a preferred brand. After all, it is better to be known as a Cadillac than as a Chevrolet. If one national group can acquire a reputation equivalent to that of a Cadillac, this would give the members of this nation not only a great deal of confidence, but it would affect their economic prospects in a very different way than would be the case if their reputation in the labor market were equivalent to that of a jalopy.

The notion of a brand name and the worship of the preferred brand as expressed in economic life thus seemed to cast a light on the preferred nationality or the preferred race. It seemed that there might be a relevant connection between the economics of competing monopolies and the endeavor of a national group to create certain monopolies for itself or its members; and I spent some years investigating problems along those lines.

The second major connection of relevance that came to me out of these experiences, was the connection between nationality and communication. If you ask what makes a person feel that he belongs to a people, is it not to some extent his ability to communicate with them? Is it not his ability to understand other persons and to predict their behavior from his own introspection? If this were so, there was a whole research area available. Can we test nationality? Under what conditions is national assimilation apt to be quick and easy and under what conditions is it apt to be slow and difficult?

Can we, in other words, get this field of national problems, nationality conflicts, and nationalism, a bit away from the heated atmosphere of special interest; can we make it accessible to the objective∙ methods which we use in other fields of science?

A third connection of relevance came in when I tried to think about the speed with which people learn to acquire a new culture or a new nationality. I had seen Czechs become Germans and Germans become Czechs; I have seen people from twenty countries in the United States become good Americans. What were the methods of this process, and what was its speed?

I gained the impression that you could measure or estimate the speed with which people came into situations where assimilation would be necessary. If you then compared this *rate of mobilization,* where they must give up many of their old habits and get new ones, with their rate of assimilation to the new culture, you could make certain quantitative statements. If people assimilate faster than they would need to, there would be no unassimilated minority in a position to make trouble; but if people get mobilized faster than they can be assimilated, they can come into towns, go to school, and learn to handle machines, only by using their own language and culture; and it is hopeless to tell them to wait until they all have learned the strange language and culture of their already well established and assimilated neighbors.

From this very sketchy approach, you can derive a whole series of research problems. How fast, how quickly, under what conditions, in which way, and with what incentives, do people learn a new culture? If you try to speed up this process, to what extent does it depend on such things as industrialization, urban growth, birth rates, or migrations, over which you have very little or no control? If we know something of these basic processes, what can we learn from them about the possibilities of national conflicts? I have written a book about this and should like to write more.

All these are problems involving judgments about relevant connections. Solutions for them sometimes just seem to come. Whether they are good solutions, I will know better in ten years than I know now. In the meantime, I can say only one thing. Such discoveries, genuine or misleading, seem to come in the form of flashes—of sudden insights. Suddenly you see two or three variables at the same time, where previously you saw them only singly. It is much the same as if you were stuck in a traffic jam, and at first you saw only the cars and houses on the two sides of one street. Now, as it were, you become capable of imagining in your mind that you are in a helicopter, and you see both of the intersecting roads at once. You see two streams of events, instead of only one. This *simultaneity* of inspection may very well be one part of the process of discovery.

Susanne K. Langer, in her book, *Philosophy in a New Key,* describes how a series of events—lines, colors, sounds—can serve as "presentational" symbols which occur at the same time. In such cases, several messages are given to you simultaneously and add up to more than if they had been given to you one by one. This "presentational" experience is part of discovery.

The other part is what has been called *insight;* it is seeing a previously unstructured process and suddenly recognizing some little part in it, or some sub-assembly in it, so well that you can pin a label on it. First you see a group of people; later on you see who is there: an old man, a woman, and three short individuals—they are probably children. You label "a father," "a mother," and "children," and you have got a picture of the inner structure of this group. Of course, your insight may be wrong, and your labels misleading, but often your labeled or structured picture is better than what you had before.

This ability to label and identify parts of a previously unidentified whole is, I think, the other part of the understanding of physical or social processes or structures. Simultaneous perception and clear, repeatable identification of parts are possibly the two main components I have found in discovery.

When do these things occur? To the best of my knowledge, they occur in moments of relaxation and release. Your chances, if your experience is at all similar to mine, of solving a problem are better under a warm shower, or playing with your children, or sitting down in an armchair and listening to music, than if you are busily digging for the answer in books—provided that you have been digging before. In such moments of release it seems as if the patterns and pieces of the puzzle are clicking into place. The answers come not when I look for them, but after I have looked for them, or before I realize that some part of my mind had been looking for them for some time.

Once an answer or a proposition comes, it is immediately recognized, but it may or may not be held securely in memory. It may disappear again, slipping back into the stream of associations, and be very hard to recapture. Problem solvers, as well as fishermen, can appreciate the truth which there may be in the tales about "the big one that got away."

Once a discovery is made and remembered, it must be followed up. This is where the old saying comes in about discoveries being one per cent of inspiration and ninety-nine per cent of perspiration. Here we meet a serious bottleneck in the lives of many people. Many of our most productive years may come at a time when we may not have the facilities to follow up the discoveries we made. Now these discoveries may be real and important, or they may be false or misleading; but in any case, many of our imaginative years come at a time when we have no facilities for testing our findings, or for following them up. Instead, we may spend the better part of a lifetime following up the ideas we had as graduate students or instructors; and even then, only following up some of them.

This has implications for the organization of research, and it has implications for the way teams can work on scientific problems.

The process of discovery is complete in any particular case only when the implications of the discovery are discovered. All true discoveries are open-ended. No discovery I can think of has been even provisionally completed before one had discovered some of the important facts which it does not explain. Only during the transition stage, when the discovery is half made, do we have the spurious feeling that it will explain or solve everything, so that we are in danger of falling victims to the arrogance of the one-idea mind. The person who comes to you with one idea, with one magical solution, is at best the person who has begun to make a discovery and has got only half-way through making it. The full discovery is not made in a flash. Rather, it is proved through its growth, although some of its critical stages may sometimes look like flashes.

Discovery is the cutting edge of a life long process of learning in every one of us, and of the age long process of learning of mankind. By seeking to see these processes as a whole, we may come to understand more about the conditions for discovery and for creative work, and perhaps more about the relation between ourselves and our minds and the universe around us.

VIII

NEWNESS OF LIFE

BY

HOXIE N. FAIRCHILD

I am not at all sure that the story which I have to tell deserves to be included in this book, for it does not concern any one illuminating moment. Things never happen to me in that catastrophic way. Even the conscious climactic period of my religious conversion occupied a whole summer. Nor does my "case," though very important to me and, thank God, to God, offer anything unusual to a student of the varieties of religious experience. Furthermore, I do not wish to use the term, "conversion," without observing that I have been a Christian all my life, for I was baptized in infancy. One could present a respectable theological case, if perhaps a slightly technical one, for regarding the moment of my baptism as the real turning point of my personal history. But a person who was baptized in 1894 and confirmed in 1934 is something of a procrastinator, and there is a great difference between receiving grace and trying to use it.

Every minute of those forty years must have done something to retard or advance the final outcome, but this little essay is not an autobiography. My baptism was largely a concession to the proprieties: nobody took it very seriously except God. I do not blame my parents for giving me practically no religious teaching or guidance as a child. The blame lies rather with the nineteenth century sentimentalism which made them liable to the fallacy that the truly spiritual person is he who refrains from believing anything in particular.

How many of the young people who are supposed to lose their faith in our "godless" colleges had any faith worth mentioning when they matriculated? The boarding school which I attended for five years was intellectually and ethically sound, but spiritually as sterile as an operating room. When I entered Columbia College in 1912 I knew practically nothing about religion, and had no religious beliefs whatever. Already conditioned to regard all problems from a secularistic point of view, by the end of sophomore year I was not only unreligious but rather aggressively antireligious—an atheist of the good old fashioned nineteenth century materialistic type.

Very clearly I remember the opinions which I held in those days, but the feelings which lent force and color to those opinions are now so deeply buried that I cannot drag them up to the surface of consciousness. So far as I can recall I was quite at ease in my unbelief and supposed that I was living a reasonably happy life. As regards moral conduct, I have nothing lurid to report for the reader's edification or entertainment. There was very little active evil and practically no good. Being a shy, sedentary, bookish youngster who had been decently brought up, I did nothing quite base enough to arouse the remorse that might have pushed me toward religion.

In the First World War I commanded an infantry platoon in France, had several narrow escapes from death, killed three men with my own hands, and lost a leg as the result of a wound received in action. None of these experiences gave me the faintest glimmer of a feeling that I wanted God or that God wanted me. It is not true that there are no atheists in foxholes: I was one of them. I went through the amputation exactly like a fox who escapes from a trap by pulling off the caught foot.

On my discharge from the army I married and began teaching at Columbia. My wife was a liberal Protestant, as she still is; but in those early days the relation between her religious beliefs and her beautiful moral character was vaguer and more tenuous than it has since become. At first she would argue with me a little, but at that time her only real arguments were feelings—feelings which I did not possess. We soon agreed to disagree on these matters, and left them in silence.

The 1920's went by without any awareness of God. Where was the need of Him? I was very happily married. Our little daughter, growing up beautifully, was a great joy to us. We had very little money, but lived comfortably enough for people of simple tastes. My war injury was no great handicap in my profession. I loved my work as teacher and scholar, and I was fairly successful in it. In short there was simply nothing to threaten the illusion of self-sufficiency.

One slight change may be worth mentioning. Although I scorned religion as much as ever, my academic specialty, the study of literature in relation to the history of ideas, compelled me to learn something about it. I did not become a real expert in the philosophy and history of religion (nor have I become one since), but almost against my will I gathered a certain amount of knowledge which was precious to me later. In a coldly objective way, I knew what religion had meant to other men long before it meant anything to me.

In 1930, I hit rock bottom for the first time: our seven year old daughter died of pneumonia. Without one thought of God, without one hope of immortality for her or for me, I sat by her bed and felt her hand growing colder, until at last the useless oxygen pump was unplugged and whirred to a stop.

But during the bitter months which followed, obscure subterranean currents began to move. The courage and goodness with which my wife rose to confront this tragedy made me wonder whether after all she did not know something of which I was ignorant. I was still far from sharing her opinions, but I thought a little wistfully of those spiritual resources which seemed to grow deeper and stronger in her with her increasing need of them. I had always been a rather coldly self-centered person with no real enemies but very few real friends. Now, in my sorrow, I found that although I had been so unloving a great many people stood ready to offer me love. Their sympathy made me feel a little ashamed of myself. It softened my cynicism and rendered me less cocksure about many things.

But I was not yet ready to make religious use of those better feelings which pain and love had given me. Instead, I was caught for some time in what I now regard as the most treacherous of all snares—the humanistic notion that the mind of man possesses autonomous power to create those values which are essential for the good

life. The feeling-tone of this theory was of course richer, more elevated, if you like, more "spiritual" than that of the drably negative
positivism which I had formerly cultivated. But that was precisely
where the danger lay: it made me suppose that I had found an
adequate substitute for religious belief.

Three years went by. I felt serene and happy when my wife and
I went off to our country home for the summer vacation of 1933.
We had completely adjusted ourselves to the loss of our child. A
second daughter had been born to us, and our faces were turned
toward the future. I was so well satisfied with my humanistic values-
philosophy that I decided to set it forth in a series of semi-popular
dialogues—a sort of literary scholar's holiday, very ripe and urbane
and quietly contemptuous both of the crass materialist and of the
bigoted supernaturalist. With three whole months ahead of me,
I should easily be able to do it.

But when I began to write I found myself in a ridiculously embar-
rassing position: I could not complete even the first page. I wanted
to affirm the creativity of the human mind. This power could hardly
exist unless man possessed some measure of free will. But although
I no longer actually thought of the universe as an automaton, I believed in no principles from which to argue that it was anything else.
If the universe were an automaton, how could it grind our human
freedom? If it were not, how could it be described without any re-
course to religious concepts? There seemed to be no earthly reason
for believing in the values in which I already did believe. Could
there be some *un*earthly reason?

Haunted by this question, I gave up my precious dialogues and
began to think about God as rationally as I could. Of course I also
began to desire God with my emotions. My thinking was certainly
wishful, but I doubt if it was more wishful than when I wished
to believe that the universe was a mechanical gadget, or when I
wished to believe that man could make spiritual values without
divine help. If there are wishes that corrupt reason, there are also
wishes that guide reason into truth. That without which reason is
impossible must somehow be reasonable.

My first step was to insist that if nature included me it must include the *whole* me—not merely the mechanisms of my body but all the powers and aspirations and potentialities which distinguish man from the lower animals. A universe thus stretched to include the human imponderables could no longer be symbolized by a machine. It seemed more rational to think of it as a fabric of thoughts proceeding from a divine creative Mind—not *my* mind. But I could not conceive of divine Intelligence without divine Wisdom, and how could there be divine Wisdom without divine Love? Moving onward in this direction I found, not without surprise, that I believed in a divine spiritual Personality Who was the source and giver of all values.

Then gradually arose a deeply painful sense of the awful apartness and differentness of this divine Personality, together with a strange feeling of kinship with Him—broken kinship, but real kinship nevertheless. By about the middle of the summer I was trying to pray to this God. Perhaps my first attempt to pray was the moment of which I have been asked to write. But it was not a moment of *discovery*—to this day I have had nothing that could be called a mystical experience. It was rather a moment of attempted self-surrender, the first willed act in a long struggle against pride which is still going on in me, and must go on until I die.

As I prayed I seemed to receive no answer at all, except for a slowly growing assurance that I was praying to an objective reality and not to a projection of my own feelings. But obviously my prayers *were* answered—otherwise I should not be writing as I am today. The great change which took place in me that summer was no accomplishment of my own. Apparently it was demanded that I make just one contribution to the process: I had to say that I wanted to find my way home. The grace needed for saying that had always been in my possession. Once I had said it, my Father saw me coming a great way off, and ran to meet me.

What remains to be said will not, I hope, be interpreted as an attempt to argue with any reader about religion. I am simply describing what happened in my own mind, without any implications as to what might happen or should happen in other minds. My beliefs are so precious to me that I can realize how precious the beliefs of other men must be to them. I have never found that the definiteness of the position at which I finally arrived has made for intolerance. On the contrary, it has drawn me into friendship and working alliance with all men who profess a positive religious faith.

Both my efforts to reason and my efforts to pray opened up the whole problem of Revelation. With religion as with everything else, I reflected, all real truth must be concrete and specific; we talk in vague abstractions only when we do not know. Would a God of love leave us completely in the dark as to the one subject which matters most for man's life? Surely He must have employed some means of showing us His nature and His will in order to enable us to draw closer to Him.

Some readers will feel that I should have been content with my initial shapeless belief in an unknowably transcendent Spirit of Love. But I found that I could not firmly believe in this without believing more than this. I must either go further or relapse into subjectivism and romantic self-worship. Once I dared to think about these matters at all, I must think onward to some objective commitment. I must never forget that I might be wrong, never presume to judge my fellow men. But, right or wrong, I must "take the leap"; I must impose my trust if I was to live at all. Merely saying, "Well, I suppose there must be Something," was intellectually spurious and emotionally impotent. In short, I saw no way of being fruitfully religious without having a religion.

By the end of that summer I regarded myself as a Christian, but I was still very hesitant to commit myself to any particular expression of the Christian faith. I felt rather superior to "mere creeds and forms." I was proud of what I had accomplished during the summer (I thought *I* had accomplished it!), proud of my new found humility, and I was inclined to think myself the only real Christian in the world.

But during the academic year 1933–1934 I continued to think and read and pray. More importantly and rather surprisingly, I condescended to worship God in the company of other Christians. In my sharp reaction against humanistic subjectivism, I found myself powerfully drawn toward a religion of sacramentally mediated grace.

I desired to be touched *from the outside* by the redeeming energy which had been set going in the world of space and time by the Incarnation. To be brought into contact with that historical event would be the closest approach to union with God that I could hope for on this side of the grave. A hostile critic of Romanticism in my personal scholarship, I was suspicious of any reliance upon an Inner Light which was not kindled and constantly rekindled from the great Outer Light. A professional rhetorician, I preferred a cult of symbolic actions to a cult of words. I felt, as I still feel, grateful to all devout and eloquent men who expound the Gospel and show us how to apply it to our own lives. But what I thought I needed even more than that was a sacramental extension of the Incarnation, a Church which inherited from Christ through His Apostles the power and the right to say to me, *"Behold* the Lamb of God! *Behold* Him, that taketh away the sins of the world!"

On the other hand, I felt that I could never guarantee absolutely unconditional obedience to the authority of the Visible Church, much less to any one of its functionaries. I believed that it was indeed guided by the Holy Spirit, but not to the exclusion of human error (and hence to the exclusion of human free will) in matters of faith and morals. It seemed to me that any uncertainties and inconsistencies in this position were inevitable characteristics of religious belief in this mortal life, where we see through a glass darkly and know only in part until that which is perfect is come.

For several months, in pursuance of these ideas and feelings, I had been attending Masses at the Church of Saint Mary the Virgin, one of the Anglo-Catholic parishes of the Episcopal Church. Of course I did not receive Communion—that would have been dishonest. But by May, 1934, I knew that I could no longer be a mere spectator. I must either share in it or go away. And it had become absolutely impossible for me to go away. Hence I made a profession of faith to Father Granville Williams of the Society of Saint John the Evangelist, who was then Rector of Saint Mary's. Under his guidance I prepared for Confirmation. I was confirmed and a few days later received my first Communion in the Advent season of 1934, just forty years and two months after my Baptism. I had wasted a great deal of valuable time. No wonder my favorite parable is that of the vineyard!

For most people who are likely to read this book, what I have had to say is an old familiar story. Probably I should not further labor the obvious by telling them what they already know about the changes which are produced in a man's life when he moves from secularism to a positive supernaturalistic religion. Excluding matters too deeply private to be spoken of in print, so far as I am concerned the great difference may be summed up in the word, "integration." When I was an unbeliever, my life was an incoherent jumble of conflicts, but since 1934 I have held a clue which makes sense of everything. A single set of principles now focuses and harmonizes my intercourse with other men, my worship, my political and social views, my philosophy of man and nature, my interpretation of history, my teaching of literature, my personal scholarship.

My application of these principles has been abysmally inadequate. Nevertheless, the mere recognition of them as goals to be striven toward, gave my life new meaning and new direction before it was too late. At least I think I know what Saint Paul means by "newness of life," and as I begin to grow a little elderly I draw deep peace from the knowledge that "newness of life" and "life everlasting" are one and the same.

IX

THE REVELATION OF HUMAN LOVE

SIMON GREENBERG

There was a time, many years ago, when I was convinced that I would be bestowing a great boon upon mankind by writing an autobiography. I was some seventeen years old then and just about emerging from an inwardly turbulent, bewildering, and at times distressing adolescence. I felt that the world needed an account of my experiences in order to save its youth from the fanciful woes to which I, as so many others of my generation, had been unnecessarily subjected.

But at that time no one asked me to write an autobiography. And now, when I am absolutely certain that my autobiography, spiritual or otherwise, has no place whatsoever on any list of the world's needs, I am asked to share with others some of my moments of discovery.

One of the Rabbis of the Talmud said of himself that even though he knew that he was not a priest, nevertheless, were his colleagues to ask him to pronounce the priestly benediction, he would do their bidding. I sometimes think that that particular Rabbi was one of my great-grandfathers, for to the best of my knowledge I never refused to do anything that any friend of mine has asked of me, if it was within my power to do it. Hence I accepted this invitation.

More than once i paid a rather exorbitantly high price for my all too ready acquiescence. But, fortunately, in the past I alone was the sufferer. Now I am afraid you will be suffering along with me. For the simple truth of the matter is that while my life has been reasonably full of activity, and has had its moments of discovery, no discovery that I have ever made was of any great direct importance to anyone but myself.

I do not belong to those rare spirits whom the Almighty chooses from time to time to be His messengers to reveal new scientific truths, new philosophical or moral insights, or new areas of esthetic appreciation. Nor did I ever live through a moment of discovery which suddenly, dramatically, and fundamentally changed the course of my life. On the contrary, to the best of my recollection, the fundamental patterns of my life developed about as normally and as smoothly as it is possible for a human life to develop. There were, to be sure, certain unexpected, unpremeditated turns in my life's path which undoubtedly left a permanent mark on all that happened to me thereafter. The opportunity, which suddenly presented itself to me while a junior at college, to leave New York and the detested daily hour and a half subway ride morning and afternoon, to spend a year in the Middle West and to attend the University of Minnesota, has remained one of the happiest memories of my life. It was the occasion for many moments of discovery. Thus also the rather casual conversation which led to an unforgettable year of travel and study in Palestine and Europe, left its effect on all subsequent events of my life.

These two highlights of my youth were in many ways of crucial significance. Neither of them, however, channelled my thoughts or energies into radically new courses. They deepened and broadened the courses along which my life had heretofore been moving, for by the time I entered college I became fully aware of the fact that my inner life was molded primarily by three factors: 1. The need for prayer. 2. The love for the Hebrew language. 3. The joy in the traditional observance of the Sabbath, Festival, and dietary laws. None of these three factors entered into my life as a result of some one moment of discovery. They grew along with me and became my most cherished and inseparable spiritual companions.

Thus there was never a time since I was a child of about six, that I did not pray daily, particularly in the morning. Nor do I ever recall that anyone ever had to remind me to say my prayers. Since I started to study Hebrew when I was about five years old, I always understood enough of my prayers to know what I was saying, and I found and continued to find the contents of the traditional daily, Sabbath, and Festival prayerbook profoundly satisfying.

As I look back over the years, I feel quite certain that whatever emotional stability I have been able to maintain, thus far, has been largely due to the period I spent daily in prayer, meditation, and study, all of which are an integral part of the traditional Jewish ritual. This I did, not because I ever had any fears of being punished either in this world or in the next. No one ever scared me with hell fire or held out promises to me of rewards in the Garden of Eden. But at a comparatively early age there was implanted within me the ineradicable feeling that one is and should live as if he is accountable for his acts.

I could not have been more than seven years old when first I heard from my Hebrew teacher the legend about the little finger of my right hand. We were being prepared for the forthcoming High Holiday season. We were reading that passage in the prayerbook which portrays the dramatic scene which takes place annually in the Court on High, where the books containing a record of each man's deeds are opened and judgment is passed on him on the basis of that record. The passage significantly stresses the thought that each man's signature is in that book, testifying to the reliability of the facts included in his record. Our teacher went beyond the mere suggestion. He told us that every night while we sleep the little finger of the right hand (for righthanded people and of the left hand, I suppose, for lefthanded people) goes to heaven to record our deeds for the day. He did not enter upon vivid detailed descriptions of punishments in store for transgressors, nor were we ever spiritually tortured with delineations of the sufferings of the evildoer. But I never forgot that story. Reinforced by daily prayer and by the teachings on every page of Scripture, it became the core around which there was developed within me an ever present sense of accountability, from which I have never emancipated myself, and hope I never will.

I add the hope, advisedly, for our Rabbis wisely warn us never to believe in ourselves until the day of our death. The science, philosophy, and psychology that I have read and studied certainly do not encourage one to believe that man is in any real sense ultimately held accountable for his deeds.

Early in my college days I was worried by the thought that in the final analysis it might be fear of what my finger was writing into the record on High that kept me from violating not only the Sabbath but also the other moral and ethical teachings of Judaism. I recalled the nights when as a youngster I would go to bed holding on to my little finger with the hope that I could keep it from going to heaven that night to make its daily report. Having studied some psychology I suspected that my observance of the religious and moral practices which I beheld widely violated by so many around me, might in reality be what so many psychologists say it is, a hangover from my childhood.

I determined, therefore, to experiment and to see whether I had the courage to violate the Sabbath. I thank God to this day that I did not decide to experiment with any principle that involved in any way the life of another human being. I remember distinctly that I was somewhat taken aback at the time by the fact that it required no particular effort on my part to spend one Sabbath as if it were not Sabbath. Much to my surprise, I found it very easy to do. I never once suffered any pang of conscience either then or thereafter. But neither did I get any particular joy out of it. I realized merely that the elimination of the Sabbath from my life created a spiritual void which was not particularly rewarding. I discovered then something which was simultaneously disconcerting and satisfying. I discovered that I could, without too much spiritual or intellectual effort, fundamentally alter the course of my life and live as if I were not a creature responsible in some unique manner for my acts. I could choose to observe or not observe the Torah. *I had all the proof I ever wanted that my will is in essence free.*

It is because I still feel that way, that I find it necessary to continue to pray that I have the wisdom and the strength to continue to direct my will along the paths that imply responsibility, accountability, and duty.

The home and environment in which I grew up were pious and

observant. My father was not a learned man—nor was my mother a learned woman. They were good people who admired learning. But I was not subjected to a consciously articulated fundamentalism. It was taken for granted that the Pentateuch was written under divine inspiration. But nobody ever insisted that I had to believe every word in it or else . . . ! Hence, when I read Ingersoll's *Mistakes of Moses* for the first time, I was amused rather than shaken. I could not quite understand why Ingersoll was so greatly concerned by those mistakes. For by that time I had studied the Prophets and Ecclesiastes. In the light of the great moral fervor and majestic visions of Isaiah and Micah, Ingersoll seemed irrelevant, and in comparison to the profound skepticism, pessimism, despair, and sense of futility that pervade Ecclesiastes, Ingersoll's doubts and questions seemed rather shallow and puerile. When, therefore, during my sophomore and junior years at college I made my first acquaintance with the theories of some of the modern biblical critics of the Graf-Wellhausian school, I found them intellectually interesting but not at all spiritually exciting.

Whether the Ten Commandments or the Law of Holiness of the nineteenth chapter of Leviticus belonged to the J or E or P document did not in any way alter my relationship to them. The modern historic approach undoubtedly helped me to reconcile my religious life with my studies in philosophy, science, and psychology. But the conflict between the two areas of interest never rose to anything like a spiritual or intellectual crisis. The two carried on within me a pleasant, stimulating, ongoing conversation which, thank God, has not yet been ended, and which, please God, never will. To keep that conversation going and yet keep it from getting out of hand, to keep it interesting and well balanced, I find daily prayer and daily periods of study and meditation indispensable.

Nor can I recall the time when I was not in love with the Hebrew language. I imagine that that was due to the fact that I prayed daily in Hebrew and that the Pentateuch was the first great book I ever read. In the small farming and summer resort community in the Catskills where I spent my early years, until my thirteenth birthday, there was no library. Until I was thirteen I never saw any English books other than the few texts we used in school, some Horatio Algers and some Frank Merriwells. Whatever there was of challenge to one's intellectual or spiritual capacities in that environment I found in the Bible and its great commentary by Rashi which I studied with a fair degree of avidity, under the tutelage of the Hebrew teacher and an uncle, who in his own way, was a unique character. He was the most learned member of that small Jewish community, uncompromisingly orthodox, intolerant, hard upon himself and upon others. He was as proud of his horses and of his ability to manipulate the new machines he was constantly buying for his farm as he was of his cantorial abilities. Every day was started very early, not only with morning prayers, but with a period of study of the Talmud. He and that community well deserve a historic monograph.

I was present, as a youngster, the night when a distillery in which he had invested his savings went up in flames. No one was permitted to do anything about extinguishing the fire or saving anything because it was the night of a religious holiday. Nor did he carry any insurance on it because he did not want ever to be suspected of having a part in a fire, should it occur. On Saturday afternoons I would join my cousins in studying with him the Pentateuchal portion of the week with Rashi's comments. It was thus that my attachments to the Hebrew language were given their deep and abiding roots.

Hence, the first book that I recall purchasing with monies that I had saved over a long period of time was a Hebrew-English dictionary. To this day, one of the greatest physical satisfactions that I enjoy is the mere handling of a newly printed Hebrew volume. Whether I intend to read it or not, I feel I get my money's worth merely by being able, from time to time, to take it off the shelf and page through it. I have tried to argue myself out of this nonrational infatuation but not with too much success.

The love of Hebrew had a profound effect upon my whole life. I knew rather early in life that I could not be permanently happy with a life's companion who did not know both English and Hebrew. Our sons were to be raised in a home that was bilingual so that from their early childhood they could use both languages with almost equal ease.

And finally I can never recall a time when I gave any serious consideration to the possibility of my abandoning the observance of the Sabbath, the Festivals, or the dietary laws. It was not a matter of grim determination. By the time I entered college I no more thought of abandoning these observances than I thought of the possibility of walking on my hands. If that meant that there were certain courses I could not take in college, certain activities I could not participate in, it did not matter. I harbored no resentment against the environment, nor against the teacher who threatened to give me no credit for a course because I refused to take the examination on a Jewish holiday. I honestly believed that was his privilege. If he wanted to exercise that privilege it was his affair and not mine.

I never experienced any serious conflict between these three fundamental patterns of my life and my interests as a member of the American generation of which I was a part. I never attended a parochial school nor ever had the desire to do so. I loved the grammar schools, high schools, and colleges which I attended. I participated in those activities in which I was most interested, such as debating, public speaking, and various literary and social problems clubs. The second book purchase which I made with joy equal to that of my purchase of the Hebrew dictionary was that of a set of the plays and sonnets of Shakespeare—in thirty-nine volumes, beautifully bound and printed, with splendid introductions and notes. I still have that set. I paid approximately five cents per volume for them, but that was some thirty-seven years ago. I never felt that Washington, Lincoln, Jefferson, or Emerson belonged to a world which was in any conflict with the world of Moses, Isaiah, Hillel, or Maimonides. They were different from one another perhaps, but only in the way in which the beauty of a sunrise differs from the beauty of a star studded sky on a moonless night. In my heart both have always lived not only at peace with one another but in intimate friendship.

The main currents of my life, therefore, flowed rather smoothly. Nevertheless, within the comparatively placid setting there were moments of illumination that not only had their immediate impact but continued to radiate for me increasing light throughout the years. They were experiences that concretized emotions that had previously been only vaguely felt and made vivid, truths that heretofore were only verbalized but never really experienced. These moments of illumination have had their perceptible effects upon my inner life, as well as upon my overt acts.

Thus I clearly recall the incident that for the first time revealed to me and made me conscious of the reality of human love. The incident was in itself not extraordinary. It occurred when I was about ten years old. My father bought me a sled, a "Fire-Fly," which, at that time, cost a dollar and a half. But I had not asked him, directly or indirectly, to buy it for me. I was old enough by then to know that it was hard enough to keep the family supplied with the barest necessities of life. Nor did I pity myself for not having a sled. I was not the only one in that sad plight. I was one of the majority. Those of us who had no sleds of their own would pull those who did have them up the hill for the privilege of riding down with the owners. One day my father saw me earning my ride. He said nothing to me but soon thereafter I had a sled.

I do not recall any gift that I ever received from anyone since then that made the same impression upon me. I am sure I did not put my feelings into words at that time. But ever since then I was absolutely certain that there are good human beings in the world and that there is such a thing as simple, unadulterated love of one human being for another. I had then no other way to explain my father's act except by assuming that he loved me. It had never occurred to me that my father owed me anything because I was his son. Nor did I, at that time, know anything about a man's need to play the hero in the eyes of his children. Since then, of course, psychologists and philosophers have tried to make me wiser and to make me believe that there is no such thing as selfless, disinterested human kindness, generosity, and love. I know the arguments and I know the proofs. But I thank God that all the mountains of evidence mustered by the wise and the learned have not been able to smother the light that was kindled in my heart in that one moment *of discovery* and illumination. It was the conscious and subconscious recollection of that moment that helped me understand that when he would say to me, "What you will do with your knowledge will be your affair, but

I would so like you to know," he had no interest at heart other than my welfare. It made it possible for me to accept gifts from him later in life with the absolute assurance that they were given in love. And I knew when as a senior at the Seminary I suggested that I would like to spend a year of study and travel in Palestine and Europe, he immediately and spontaneously offered his hardearned savings to pay for all my needs, that it was that same love that had brought the sled to me years back which was again speaking.

It was that experience which in my life laid the foundations for my unwavering faith and conviction that human beings can be and are moved to act from motives of love, and that our greatest need as human beings is to be both the objects of the love of other human beings and the bestowers of love upon them. That was my first conscious encounter with love and it opened the door for me to the most beautiful and most challenging of all of the experiences beckoning the human spirit.

My first conscious encounter with "ambition" took place in my eighth year in public school when we were studying Shakespeare's *Julius Caesar*. At that time it was an encounter with the word only— but not with its substance. You remember Brutus's emphasis on Caesar's ambition and Mark Anthony's sardonic references to Brutus's accusations. As a youngster I mouthed the word but never really knew what it meant. I had never heretofore experienced anything that I could identify as ambition. I did not have to wait very long, however, for that experience.

I recall vividly the first general assembly when as a freshman I sat in the crowded auditorium of the high school and listened to the editor of the school paper speak to us from the platform, urging us to buy our copies of *The Recorder*. Suddenly, and for no good reason that I could recall, I felt a keen all pervading desire to be able to stand on that platform and speak to an audience. I did not believe that I could ever do it. But I was determined to try. I was sure then that nothing would give me greater satisfaction than attaining this goal. I set myself to the task and some two years later my first keenly felt ambition was fulfilled. I triumphed in a semi-annual oratorical contest. But the reaction was almost immediate. That very night though I walked home elated, it was an elation shot through with a sense of emptiness. I had attained my ambition but did not experience the substantial joy I had anticipated.

I never forgot that. All of my readings and meditations since then on the vanity of personal human ambitions have been illuminated, made real and tangible by that early, poignant experience of disillusionment in the moment of triumph. Whatever modest triumphs came since then were made the sweeter because they were not previously passionately sought, nor was the measure of their joy calculated in anticipation, nor could another man's triumph ever again make me unhappy with my own lot. I have been forever grateful for that first early and essentially insignificant incident which helped me discover, without causing too much pain at the time, the truth of the biblical proverb—that "in the midst of laughter the heart aches." That illumination, I feel, has kept me from walking down many an alley leading to false ambitions and bitter disillusionments.

It was about the same time that something happened which opened up for me one of those unhappy aspects of human nature which cause endless and unnecessary human suffering. I refer to the almost universal human tendency to ascribe motives to the acts and words of others and then to judge them on the basis of those ascribed motives. Again it was an incident which intrinsically was of the very least significance. But it somehow managed to shock me in a manner that made it one of the indelible experiences of my life.

My closest friend during high school days was one of the most active leaders of the student body, occupying at one time or another all of the choice posts coveted by the average student. We were almost inseparable during that period. One morning while going from one classroom to another, I asked another acquaintance whether he had seen my friend. His response was unexpectedly sharp and caustic. "Sure I saw him," he said, "but he never says good morning to anybody." His voice and words carried in them the sharp hurt that anyone feels who believes himself to be snubbed or wilfully insulted. I knew my friend, and I was certain as one ever could be of anything that he never wittingly meant to hurt anyone. At first I felt hurt at the implied insult to my friend. But as time passed and I had occasion to observe human beings I realized that there had opened before me at that moment that vast abyss of human evil and suffering due to our inveterate inclination to read the other man's mind, to attribute evil motives to others, and to judge them on the basis of what we attribute to them. I have often been tempted over the years to try to puzzle out why "A" acted thus and so toward me and "B" in yet another way. But I never permitted myself to spend too much time in such vain searches. The caustic answer I received to a simple question in the hallway of a high school while going from one class to another always reverberates anew in my ears, and I desist. It has been a light that has saved me from many a heartache and helped me avoid many a stumbling block in my path.

But one more moment of discovery. When I look back over my life I utter a special prayer of gratitude that I rarely had occasion to witness the depths of human evil. I had read about it in the newspapers, but those among whom I grew up never quarreled bitterly, at least not in my hearing nor to my knowledge, nor did anyone ever harm another person out of sheer human cussedness. I knew also that there was such a thing as antiSemitism, but I never saw any real expressions of it, despite the fact, or perhaps because of the fact that I had grown up in a farm community where Jewish and non-Jewish children sat in the same small classroom, played games together, fought and laughed together as children, and nothing more. It was not until I was at college in 1920–1921 that I unwittingly looked into the dark pit of human hate. The *Dearborn Independent* was spewing forth its venom at the time. But I was not upset by what was being written. The thing did not seem real to me. Then one day I found the magazine in a barber shop and as I sat down on the barber's chair I altogether innocently remarked, "I wonder what the *Dearborn Independent* wants of the Jews." The answer was a veritable avalanche of abuse and hate, the kind I had never heard before nor even imagined possible. And the barber said it all spoken quietly, while cutting my hair. I was too stunned to say or do anything, but walked out a much sadder individual. Here was a human being who to all appearances was sane, normal, and civilized yet harbored insane, irrational hate.

Some years later I came upon a British policeman in one of the alleys of Jerusalem as he was beating an Arab. It was not the beating itself that distressed me but the calm, cold expression on the policeman's face. He was no more emotionally touched by what he was doing than if he were beating the dust out of a rug. Again the light was turned on for me, so that I caught a glimpse into the dark recesses of the human soul—its capacity to indulge in hate for its own sake as it does in love, and its ability to observe human suffering without wincing.

I do not know if all of us have to go through the experience of discovering the reality of human love and human hate. I know that to me these were mere words until the moment when I experienced them not only with my mind but with my whole being. And what I saw in other men's hearts I learned also to recognize in my own. Only then did I begin to understand the full import of the Rabbinic injunction that it is incumbent upon man daily and constantly to stimulate his good inclination over against his evil inclination, lest the evil in him overwhelm him.

These then are a few of those moments in which sudden and fairly intense light was shed for me upon some of the abiding aspects of human life. As I was writing this paper I recalled with gratitude many more such moments. No discovery I mentioned in it was associated with prayer or study or home life. Some came to me as a boy while bringing cows home from pasture, others while pondering a text of the Bible or of Rabbinic literature, or while reading some favorite poet or philosopher, or while observing the growth and development of our two children, or while meditating on the infinite blessings that have come from a life of loving companionship with the sweetheart of one's youth. Such moments, I am sure, must be numerous in the life of all of us. They are the little candles kindled for us by the grace of God, to light the vast spaces of our minds and souls. They are God's gifts to those of us who are not destined by Him to be the media through which the great and sudden bursts of light occasionally illumine the life of the whole human race.

It takes a great number of candles to equal the illumination of a streak of lightning. But perhaps there is some comfort in the thought that the light furnished by candles is never blinding, and by and large is far more steady and dependable.

X

THERE IS ONLY ONE ROAD TO PEACE

BY

REX STOUT

From 1941–1945 I was Chairman of the Writers' War Board. On that Board 6,400 American writers were registered with us, and each week we would get an average of 120 requests for pieces of writing from the Treasury Department, the Army, the Air Force, the Navy, all departments of government, and many other kinds of organizations that were fighting the war. We might get a request for a half-dozen so-called slogans from the Air Force to persuade pilots not to do certain things, or we might get a request, and we did get a total of about sixty requests during the war for whole books, and about twenty-nine of them got written.

Anyway, for those years in my functioning as Chairman of the Writers' War Board, and dealing through the Board with 6,400 American writers, I had only one thing to do. The only thing I had to do was to try my best to help to get American writers to write something in any way they could to get more Germans and Japanese and Italians killed. That is what it amounted to, and for a man all of whose eight great-grandparents had been Quakers, for such a man that was a rather curious enterprise. And one day when I was thinking about the anomaly, in fact, the incongruity of that function of mine, it occurred to me that there has never been any successful effort to create a community of men and women, no matter how small or how large, within which organized violence is not to be permitted, that is, a peaceful community, without calling upon and using three things, three elements: morality, education, and law.

There is not a single case from all of the history we have from the most primitive tribes up to today and the most complex and immense political organisms, there is not a single recorded instance of the establishment of a peaceful community, no matter what the size, no matter what the culture, no matter what the stage of civilization, without all three of those elements being present: morality, education, and law.

If human civilization, human experience, has proved any single statement about man as a political animal—if any one statement has been proved over and over again without a single exception, it is that one. After that thought occurred to me that day I went to a good deal of trouble to try to check it because it seemed to me to offer the only solid basis for any attempt to make the world a peaceful community. I checked it with a great many different kinds of people, with a lot of books, with jurists, and historians, and educators, and so far as I know, and so far as all of the people whom I have asked about it know, that statement is unexceptionally true.

If it is, then any talk about a peaceful world, any advocacy of a peaceful world, any wishing for a peaceful world, without including in your program world law, a limited world government, is intellectually either dishonest or incompetent and is actually amoral; that is, it has no moral significance at all because it has no function. It has no reality.

There have been, we all know, many attempts not only to create the desire for but to impel the start toward a peaceful world, peace on earth, by moral argument. No one realizes more keenly than I do the necessity of the moral urge, of the moral sense, in trying to create a peaceful world; but if history has shown us anything about a peaceful world, it is that all of the attempts to educate the people of the world to a desire for peace on earth, and all of the attempts to intensify in their breasts the moral urge toward a peaceful world have certainly been and are doomed always to be failures unless we bring into the world, as we have into every other community, the concept of law and the use of law.

So that is why active advocates of world government say that no man or woman really has any moral right to pretend to be an advocate of peace on earth unless he or she is at the same time an advocate of a world government.

If you once accept that basic fact—that we cannot have world peace without world law—you go on from there, of course, to study the matter and to become active in that phase of the problem which most appeals to you and in which you feel you are best capable of functioning.

Probably the best way to do that is to ask one of the many questions that arise, one of the many difficulties that are present the minute you decide that world peace is worth the sacrifices we would have to make in order to get world government. At once you run into fascinating political questions, such questions as: "Would the world legislature be unicameral or bicameral?" Or this one: "Whether the world parliament, the world legislature were unicameral or bi-cameral, how would you decide how the different peoples and nations of the world are to be represented in that world legislature?"

Of course, as we are Americans and believe in the basic concepts and ideals and processes of American Democracy, naturally we would say right off that each people, each nation, would be represented in a world legislature in proportion to its population, because that is one of the basic concepts of the American democratic process. But with a little thought you realize the concrete defects of such an arrangement. For instance, if the United States of America and India were both in this government, India's voice would be twice as large, twice as powerful, as that of the United States. Well, maybe theoretically that is all right. Morally, ideally, certainly by the democratic theory it is all right, but actually in order to get world government we have got to have a majority of the people of the United States wanting it, and a majority of the people in the United States wanting it have got to persuade our national Congress to support it, to get behind it, to see that we get a world government and we are members of it. And it would be impossible to get either a majority of the American people or a majority of either branch of our Congress to get behind the idea of establishing a limited world government, if India has twice as large a representation or voting power in the world legislature as this country.

So we begin to consider other proposals, proposals that, in addition to population, the voting strength of each country, each people, be based partly on population, partly on the national income, partly on industrial power, partly on either existing or potential military power, partly on something else. There have been several explorative bases suggested on which we should arrive at some allocation of the voting power in the world legislature. The most interesting one, I think, is that literacy, the percentage of literacy in each country would be one of the major factors in determining the voting strength of a country in the world government.

If you got interested enough in world government to spend a little of your time, or much of your time, working for it, the question that would interest you most might be, "What about Russia?" "How can we talk about a world government in the present condition of the world, divided as it is into two camps?" We suggest establishing the world government under the provisions of Article 109 of the United Nations Charter, which provides not only that the charter may be amended at any time but also that in the year 1955, whether any country has asked for it or not, a meeting of the General Assembly is to be held at which the revision of the charter shall be on the agenda. There is no provision in the present charter saying how much it must be amended or indeed that it must be amended at all, but it does say that a proposal to amend or revise the charter must be on the agenda of the General Assembly in 1955. If and when an attempt is made to revise the United Nations charter so as to make it a constitution for a limited world government, either in 1955 or earlier, then the Russian representatives in the General Assembly and the satellite countries' delegates would join in that attempt or they would not. If they did not join, they would not take part in that process. They would be out of it right from the beginning.

Let us say, however, that they would join in the discussions and in the attempt to revise the charter even if only to try to sabotage it, and the revision is finally agreed upon by a two-thirds vote of the General Assembly. In the approval of the revised charter by the General Assembly the attitude of Russia and her satellites, while it certainly would be important and most interesting, would actually have no legal bearing, because if a two-thirds vote of the General Assembly approved the revised charter, that would be settled, it would be approved, and would go to the member nations for ratification.

If Russia did not remain in the United Nations reformed into the world government, the point where Russia probably would fall out would be this next point where ratification is required. There are different constructions placed on this. Different lawyers say different things about it. But probably ratification by three-fourths of the member nations would actually establish the revised charter and put the United Nations in operation under that revised charter.

Then what if Russia and its satellites refused to accept that new United Nations with that revised charter and get out, what do the advocates of world government say would happen? We say this, if you had fifty or more countries ratifying and going along with the establishment of a limited world government, obviously it would not be preposterous to call it a world government and you would do so and go ahead, just as this country went along for two years and a half as the United States of America, although one, Rhode Island, had not ratified. (By the way, I am not comparing Rhode Island to Soviet Russia.)

Anyway, if there were fifty or more countries in, it would certainly not be silly to call it a world government. You could do so and you could proceed. If there were only fifteen in, obviously it would be nonsense to call it world government. You would not have accomplished anything except the discussion that would have taken place. In between the fifteen and the fifty? I do not know. It would have to be decided at that time whether or not it would be sensible to call it a world government if you had thirty, thirty-five, forty, forty-five. At what point would it become foolish to call it a world government? How low would you have to go, or how high would you have to go?

Now, what do we mean by limited world government? We mean a government with all of the powers of a government in order to function effectively; that is to say, it would have its own police force, it would have its own constitution, the revised charter of the United Nations, it would have its own legislature, its own executives, its own judiciary; but in the operation of all of those powers it would be limited to dealings either with nations or with individuals in so far as their activities broke the peace of the world or threatened the peace of the world.

I am often asked exactly how do you limit the powers of such a government to those fields, as you have described, without the danger that the government itself, being once established, would overstep the boundaries and would invade portions of our conduct and of our national interest that we would not want to be invaded? And that is one of the questions that I always have to decline to try to answer because it is so highly technical and highly legal, and I am not a lawyer.

All I know is that every competent lawyer who has interested himself in the problem of world government and who has made an effort to write a proposed wording of the constitution for one—all of them claim that it can be done. The one whose opinion in the matter I know most about in detail, and whose opinion in a way for different reasons I respect most, is Associate Justice William O. Douglas of the United States Supreme Court, and he is completely convinced that it can safely be done.

Out of the some two or three thousand difficult and vital questions connected with the establishment of a world government in order to prevent World War III, and in order to get a peaceful world community, out of the two or three thousand such questions, I have tried very sketchily to deal with eight or nine. The other 3,417 will have to be left for some other time.

XI

THE AUTHOR MUST FIND HIS PROPER ANCESTRY

BY

VAN WYCK BROOKS

It was in Dresden when I was thirteen years old that my mind first came to life. I had been taken by my mother to the Zwinger, the lovely Baroque building that has since been demolished, and there I saw the great picture collection that has vanished into Russia and that I almost learned by heart. For, having gone there once, I went back every morning for three or four months, so that for years afterwards I could close my eyes and see all the pictures on half the walls. From that day forward through the rest of a year, when I was approaching fourteen, wherever I happened to be, for a week or a month, in Vienna, Rome, Florence, Naples, Paris, or London, I spent every morning in a picture gallery, roaming about from room to room, with a neophyte's zeal for the religion of the history of art.

Reading again, not long ago, the *Praeterita* of Ruskin, I discovered that this idol of my childhood had been also thirteen when he was awakened mentally, as I was, by a book—in his case, by Samuel Rogers's *Italy,* with vignettes by Turner, in my case by Mrs. Jameson's *Italian Painters.* For this book confirmed the feeling that I had derived from the pictures themselves, starting me on a course of reading that—to quote Ruskin's phrase—"determined the main tenor of my life." This popular nineteenth century handbook was my open sesame, and I might not have read Berenson if I had not read this. I might not even have discovered Ruskin, the favorite author of my whole adolescence, who illumined economics as well as art for me;

for *Munera Pulveris* and *Unto This Last* were to affect me later as
much as the Italian studies affected me at first. To what fortuitous or
trivial events, as they may seem, when one looks back, one owes
perhaps this first awakening, a view, a book, a face in the street that
strikes a prepared sensibility with the force of a mystical message that
kindles the mind. It may be a square of yellow light on a dusty floor
on a morning in spring, seen for the first time in the year, exciting the
eye, that suddenly turns a boy into a landscape painter, opening a
new world of desire for him. Up to that time, for my part, I had
collected birds' nests merely, pestering the birds themselves by steal-
ing their eggs. It was my brother who had been the reader and who
had been found at three or four reading Macaulay's history upside
down.

As for Ruskin, I even unknowingly followed him in attempting
to make pencil drawings of pictures in museums. One of these was
Fra Angelico's "Crucifixion" in the Louvre, where Ruskin on his
first visit to the continent, had made his first sketch. He had drawn
Rembrandt's "Christ at Emmaus," obtaining a permit so to do, while
I was stopped by one of the guards and told that the lowest age limit
for this, whatever the case may have been, was now fifteen. Ruskin
had become an admirable artist, as one sees in the drawings he made
for his books, while I had no luck at all with my few efforts, sketching
Roman ruins, street scenes and what not; and moreover I outgrew the
wish to write the art criticism that I loved and turned to another
branch of this kind of writing. Not only was I never an art critic but
I had an almost morbid dread of so much as attempting to write
about painting and painters, although I have known more painters
even than writers and although from the first I was convinced that
criticism in some form was the most delightful activity one could
dream of in this world. I even felt that everything might be expressed
in criticism, as others have felt about music or fiction or sculpture—
in the last case, Michelangelo, as everyone knows; and certainly
Ruskin, for one at least, expressed in criticism a good half dozen
sides of life.

Meanwhile, Ruskin drew me to shelves of art historians, who
drew me into the study of history as well, and presently theology,

from the Flanders of Thomas à Kempis to Cardinal Newman and even Jonathan Edwards. By gradual steps I became a literary and social critic, concerned rather with the present and the future than the medieval past, and especially concerned with America where so many writers somehow fail to *pass beyond* their "moments of discovery." And what, after all, is the value of these moments if they do not lead to a further evolution, if they are not merely the first of a series of steps?—a question that greatly interests me and that I trust may interest you, the question of the arrested development of American writers.

For our literature is a literature of boys, it has often been said. Many of our classics have survived as classics for boys, or one might better say that Cooper, Irving, Longfellow, Dana, the author of *Two Years Before the Mast,* have largely survived as classics for adolescents. T. S. Eliot has plausibly found a lack of the maturity in Poe that "comes only with the maturing of the man as a whole," and certain it is that, like Mark Twain in quite another way, Poe is preeminently a writer for adolescents. Was there not something of the boy-philosopher in William James, moreover, the philosopher who was once asked to be "serious for a moment"?—and is this not even one of James's charms?—while many writers of more recent years have suggested overgrown exuberant boys, John Reed, for one, the "playboy of the Russian revolution." Jack London played outlaw and pirate to the end of his life, and Sherwood Anderson's adolescent gropings were matched by those of Thomas Wolfe, a writer of genius who never quite grew up. Then there was Vachel Lindsay, adolescent from first to last, and Mencken, who has so often suggested "Peck's Bad Boy." What has been said of our civilization, that it was always beginning again, at the same level, on each new frontier, might perhaps be said of our literature also. It is always beginning again as adolescent.

True, or half true, as this is, there might be nothing regrettable in it if writers, remaining "young," remained buoyant and vital, as E. E. Cummings remains buoyant and vital, the poet who has retained for thirty years the freshness, the gaiety, the wonder, the curiosity of youth. For the rest, the youthfulness of the American mind, its adventurousness and zest, has been the great gift of America to the older countries, and one might ask why America should not remain adolescent—is not a high spirited boy better than a tired old man? But, good as the traits of youth may be, it is not good to be immature when this means the arrested development that is common with our writers, when "incompleteness" and "truncation," as Irving Howe says, have been "so pervasive" in our culture. Mr. Howe, writing on Sherwood Anderson, observes, as many have observed before, that "the early achievement of American writers" is "seldom enlarged in maturity," while he dwells on the "bewilderment" and the "disappointment" of Anderson himself when Thomas Wolfe brutally told him that he was "finished." This has been for thirty years almost a commonplace of American critics, who have said that, with us, the abortive career is the rule, that something "happens" to American writers, that their talents fizzle out, that "there are no second acts in American lives." How many writers have realized themselves that they were "prematurely cracked, like an old plate," as Scott Fitzgerald put it? As the young writer says in Saroyan's *The Assyrian and Other Stories,* "Exuberance did the trick, but now it doesn't. . . . It did the trick for Thomas Wolfe, as long as he lived, and for a lot of others too, but exuberance seems to stop when a man gets past his middle thirties, or the man himself stops." Saroyan is saying of the American writer what Mrs. Lightfoot Lee said in Henry Adams's novel long ago, "You grow six inches high and then you stop. Why will not somebody grow to be a tree and cast a shadow?" In *Green Hills of Africa,* Hemingway said much the same thing: "Something happens to our good writers at a certain age." Hemingway added, "We do not have great writers. . . . We destroy them in certain ways."

But is it true that "we" destroy them? Is not this a fallacy which has also become a commonplace of American critics? I cannot feel as I used to feel when I wrote *The Ordeal of Mark Twain* that writers fail because of external conditions, because "we" or their wives and their friends destroy them, or editors, or publishers, or the pressure of the world they live in, or public opinion. It is largely an illusion that writers "fall" to Hollywood or Broadway as women who stooped to folly were once said to fall; for is this not often, at least, with writers, a question rather of finding their natural level? No, serious writers seldom fall, at least in any significant sense, nor can it be said properly that "we" destroy them, although without doubt they *are* destroyed because they are thwarted as writers, even to the point where they lose the will to live. That there is a talent which is "death to hide," which, hidden, or balked, or undeveloped, brings on death, innumerable writers have shown in America, as elsewhere. Was not Jack London's suicide plainly a result of this frustration, like Vachel Lindsay's suicide, like Hart Crane's later?— as, ordered to stop drinking, Scott Fitzgerald drank all the more, said one of his friends, because he did not "wish to get well."

But what are we asking for? Do we Americans expect too much when "normally," as Sainte-Beuve remarked, "fifteen years constitute a literary career"? Is it not known that under the best conditions many writers are nervously exhausted in the middle of their lives? Have not defeat, disease, disappointment, and early death character- ized the lives of writers in all times and countries? The literary temperament is prone to the stresses and strains that have made the "calamities of authors" everywhere a byword; and yet the complaints of so many Americans can scarcely be ignored, nor can the evidence of so many American lives. That American talent fails to mature in countless cases we all know, and, if this is not because "we" destroy it, what can be the reason unless that the talent is destroyed by the writers themselves? That this is the case, in fact, Hemingway says in another of his stories, referring to the young writer in *The Snows of Kilimanjaro,* "He had destroyed his talent himself. Why should he blame this woman because she kept him well? He had destroyed his talent by not using it, by betrayals of himself and what he believed in, by drinking so much that he blunted the edge of his perceptions, by laziness, by sloth and by snobbery, by pride and by prejudice, by hook and by crook. It was a talent all right but instead of using it he had traded on it." There are surely plenty of reasons here to explain the "truncation" of American talents in this or that or the other of a hundred cases, and they all boil down to a generaliza- tion of another remark of Scott Fitzgerald, "I had been only a mediocre caretaker of my talent." True or not in Fitzgerald's case, this is surely true in scores of others, and inevitably it leads one to the question, What is a *good* caretaker of one's talent? The biblical parable of the talents, referring to money, is equally germane in this other connection, the psychological problem of the writer's life.

This is one of the weightier matters that critics have ignored in their recent preoccupation with the mint and cumin, the grammatical and rhetorical minutiae of literary texts, concerned as they are with form alone, with "the letter that giveth life"—T. S. Eliot's reversal of the words of the gospel. For have not the new critics devoted to craftsmanship so much zeal that they have had none to spare for other questions? How many writers' conferences, how many summer schools, how many classes, how many books and magazines dwell each year, with fanatical concentration, on the "form" of writing, never diverting a moment's thought from the question, "How to write well," to the question, "How to live well to be a writer?" Who ever speaks of the kind of life that writers should lead to become great writers or the way to use their energy to develop their powers? Who considers what taking good care of one's talent means? Who thinks of maturity as desirable or worthy of study? The cult of youth that has dominated writers since even before the First World War, from Edna Millay to Hemingway and Fitzgerald, has filled them with a fear of growing old that almost precludes at the outset any regard for the uses of growing up. Concerned with literary technique alone, oblivious of what might be called the more important technique of literary living, they are apt to end with the feeling of Fitzgerald in *The Crack-Up*—the "feeling that I was standing at twilight on a deserted range, with an empty rifle in my hands and the targets down."

But what is growing up? What does growth mean with a man who is a writer? Is this not a question of the art of literary living? When I was the literary editor of *"The Freeman,"* thirty years ago, there was a French writer, Jules Bois, living in New York, who used to come into my office to discuss a book he proposed to write and publish perhaps as a serial in our weekly paper. After writing about Mark Twain myself, I was full of the question of the American

writer and why so many talents fizzled out here, why so many
American careers seemed to be abortive and why American writers
lived so blindly. It was obvious to me that Jules Bois's project would
throw some light on this, for he intended to show what a fully
developed career might be and what steps a writer might take in
order to achieve it. His subject and his title were suggested by *The
Imitation of Christ,* which he always carried about in his pocket with
him, and Jules Bois hoped to parallel this *vade mecum* of the
Christian life with a manual of the literary life for the guidance of
writers. In planning *The Imitation of Goethe* he felt that this greatest
of Germans had known, and possibly better than anyone else, how a
writer can best coin the metal that is in him, how he should live in
order to make the best use of all his powers, how meet, for this
purpose, the various contingencies of life. Where should a writer
live, what people should he choose to know, how should he travel,
how read, how divide his hours, how regulate his habits, his appetites,
his interests, his passions? While Jules Bois was well aware that
writers can scarcely be classified, that they are more individualized
than other types, he knew they had certain characteristics and needs
in common, and, aware as well of the powerful role that emulation
plays in life, he felt that Goethe might serve them in a way as a model.

That book Jules Bois never wrote, but when, along with all the
world, I discovered Albert Schweitzer, I found that in a sense this
great man had written it for him. For Schweitzer related how he
had imitated Goethe, finding in him a model on many occasions.
Having doubts himself about studying medicine, he had seen how
Goethe allowed Wilhelm Meister to become a surgeon and how
Goethe, too, for peremptory reasons, abandoned other work to return
to the natural sciences at a certain moment. Schweitzer, obliged to
labor at accounts when his mind was full of other plans, was able
to remember Goethe spending hours straightening out the finances of
a small German state; while, as a young man, he had been struck by
Goethe's account in the *Harzreise* of a journey he had made through
November mist and rain. Goethe had visited with "suitable help"
a minister's son who was in "spiritual difficulties," and thereafter,
when Schweitzer had to undertake some irksome task, he would

say to himself, "There is a *Harzreise* for you." He had found Goethe haunted by anxiety about justice, and, reduced himself to despair in Africa, he could think of Goethe's last plan for Faust, to win back land from the sea on which men might live. Then, remembering the vigorous eager way in which Goethe shared the life of his age in its thought and its activity alike, Schweitzer felt standing beside him in the forest this "man who really understood" and who had so often been his model.

It is true enough that Schweitzer is a writer of a special type, apparently as remote as possible from Scott Fitzgerald, but, if not a great writer, he is a great man writing, and humanly mature, as Goethe was. Goethe's life, besides, had other aspects in which other types can find their own tendencies corroborated and, if need be, corrected, and he has in fact served as a model for many writers. For is not the instinct of emulation one of the strongest in imaginative minds and perhaps the most powerful force in a writer's education? Everyone remembers how, as a boy, Alexander Pope dreamed of seeing Dryden whom at last he saw and whom he regarded as poetry in a bodily form, as Dostoievski's first act on visiting St. Petersburg, still a boy, was to seek out Pushkin's old chambers and the site of his duel. Dostoievski would have put on mourning at the news of Pushkin's death if he had not been wearing it already for his mother, expressing the mood of hero worship that writers naturally feel in their youth and that springs from their need of models to shape their careers. Our age has had small faith in heroes because it has seen so many false heroes, the Hitlers and Mussolinis who have been tribal idols, and it inherits, moreover, the mood of the "debunkers." But has not William Carlos Williams said that the "example" of Henri Fabre has "always stood beside" him "as a measure and a rule"? "It has made me quiet," Williams says, "and induced in me a patient industry and . . . a long-range contentment"; and was it not partly Fabre's example that "behooved" him to "be at one's superlative best" and to "work single-mindedly for the task"? That hero worship still exists, although it is not recognized and operates behind a screen, as one might say, one can see in the deep South where Faulkner's example and presence have given birth to a whole school of writers. For we must have models in our minds to discipline ourselves, images of the kind of perfection we wish to attain, and writers have always attested that these models are necessary to serve them as pacemakers and criteria for their development and growth. The only question for a given writer is to have the models that are best *for him,* that will forward his own particular development and growth.

If American writers fail to develop, if, so often, they fail to grow, is not this therefore a question that one ought to examine? Have these writers lacked models, or have they followed the wrong models, and in any case what is the reason for it? When, speaking of William James, whom he did not consider a true philosopher, Santayana suggested that, in his youth, James had never seen a philosopher "whom he would have cared to resemble," this writer was rash perhaps on two accounts. For, in the first place, James was undoubtedly a true philosopher, and moreover he had seen Emerson, whom he admired immensely. But how right is this point of Santayana in other connections. How many living American writers have grown up in a world that afforded no hint of a model for their emulation, so that in their youth they never saw a writer whom they would have "cared to resemble" and scarcely heard of one in their country or their region? And was it not natural that, driven abroad for their models they should sometimes have followed models who were not good *for them?*

But what is a "good" model? Does one mean a good man in the sense of the old Chinese painter, "If one's moral character is not high one's art will correspondingly lack style"? Milton corroborated this when he said that a writer "ought himself to be a true poem" if he "wishes to write well . . . in laudable things"; and of what was Gauguin thinking when he said, "With the masters I converse. Their example fortifies me. When I am tempted to falter I blush before them"? Was he not referring to personal nobility also, or at least to the "conscience" and "patience" that Rodin described as the two fundamental traits of the life of an artist? But if this were taken to mean that the writer must be a good man in the ordinary sense, that his nature must be harmonious, it would be far too simple, for there must be, as AE said, all manner of contraries in a writer's nature to intensify the interaction of his faculties and parts. I remember an eminent English critic saying to me once, "Have you noticed that the best men are sometimes the worst writers and that sometimes the best writers are the worst men?" I had noticed this indeed, though it never made me happy, as it seems to make those who believe in "salvation by sin." How often one is obliged to notice it! Was not Cicero, unquestionably great as a writer, in his personal nature a double-dealer, treacherous, unscrupulous, a braggart, a coward, and a liar, as his latest editor proves from the evidence of his letters, and in how many writers has one found the kind of disruption and conflict out of which have sprung great works of the imagination? For there must be darkness in literature as well as light, descents into hell as well as paradises, a fact we are not likely to forget at a time when Rimbaud and Baudelaire have played so large a part in the minds of writers. At this time when life itself has seemed the "dark dream" of which Rimbaud wrote, it is natural that these two poets have been so magnetic and that Rimbaud has been the idol of literary youth all over the world, the voice of its impatience with the past and its impulse of destruction. He was a great virtuoso at a moment when virtuosity seemed more important than ever to the literary mind, one of the word-revolutionists whose verbal and technical innovations outrivalled those of Pound later and possibly Joyce. He, too, had descended into hell like millions in a warsick world, like thousands of sensitive minds who shared his disillusion with the standards of civilization that was wrecking the world and who found in him both a prophet and a brother, another "man who really understood."

Thus Rimbaud became a model for the twentieth century literary mind as Goethe had been universally a century before, and for much the same reason, odd as it seems, because the main object of both these poets had been to develop their faculties to the highest degree. For to become a seer was Rimbaud's aim in all he did, and this had been the aim of Goethe also, while the intensity with which both pursued it explained their power over other minds, irrespective of all the immeasurable differences between them. Both had followed models before they were models themselves in turn, and Rimbaud's special model was Baudelaire, who had said it was through dreaming that man entered into communication with the rich dark world that surrounds him. It was to see in this dark world that Rimbaud used all known means to induce in himself the state of perpetual dreaming, and he supposed he was following his master in depraving himself deliberately by what he called the "derangement of all the senses." He believed that one could not become a seer without transcending the old conceptions of humanity, of good and evil, and in order to make his work as an artist his sole and only virtue he consciously sought what he called "monstrosity of soul." But this was not only remote from Goethe's conception of becoming a seer, it was equally remote from Baudelaire's, for Rimbaud had never seen the letters in which, by implication, Baudelaire passionately repudiated just this notion. Far from approving of what, to him, were weaknesses and vices, he described his horrified struggles to cast them off, regarding the taking of drugs, which he tried, as no less immoral than suicide, and rejecting the "artificial paradises" to which they led. Not to be willing to accept what he described as the conditions of life was to betray one's soul, Baudelaire said, and he would have been the first to add that, as a model, Rimbaud was good only for the "devil's party." For he did not wish to belong to this party himself.

There are excellent authorities for those who feel that one *should go* to the devil if one's deepest convictions and impulses lead that way, and Rimbaud possessed, as a writer, the "conscience" and even the "patience," perhaps, that made him a good model from Rodin's point of view. But, in this connection, a further question arises. What is the nature of the disciple who follows the model? For, in any given case, a model must be *congruous* before it can be described as a good model, one that is not discordant with one's own personal aptitudes, one's mental conformation and essential aims. This is the question that involves so many American writers and the models they have followed mistakenly so many times, as it seems obvious that, for one, Hart Crane was mistaken in following Rimbaud when he wished to write a great poem in the tradition of Walt Whitman.

Yvor Winters, writing on Crane, suggests that he followed the model, or followed at least the counsel, of Whitman himself, saying that the doctrines of Whitman, and Emerson, if really put into practice, would naturally lead a man to suicide. What we appear to have, says Winters, is "a poet of great genius who ruined his life and his talent by living and writing as the two greatest religious leaders of our nation recommend," for did they not say that men should cultivate all their impulses, and what, in the end, could be more suicidal than this? But when one thinks of Emerson, with all his checks and balances, and of Whitman's "clear sun shining" and "fresh air blowing," one feels compelled to look for another explanation—for whoever committed suicide by following these?—and was not Rimbaud "constantly" in Hart Crane's mind during the months when, as Philip Horton says, he was planning *"The Bridge"?* Whom was he following when, as this biographer observes, he cultivated "on principle" homosexuality and alcoholism, "cultivated them assiduously," though he did not enjoy his descent into hell and felt that he was really a martyr to it? That Crane actually "adopted" Rimbaud's "method" of living, with the same object in view, Brom Weber says, in his more recent biography of Crane—although Rimbaud despised all the ideas that Crane was trying to realize, the Whitmanian ideas he was endeavoring to embody in *"The Bridge."* Did not Rimbaud wish to "sell" democracy "if anyone would take it"? No poets were ever more antithetic in everything they had to say than Rimbaud, with his disgust for the "human pigs," for "justice, republics and peoples . . . *périssez! . . . passez!"* and Whitman whose whole aim was to celebrate these; and could there have been a more fatal conflict for a man who wished to sing the "Bridge"—the "American myth"—of which Whitman "flung the span"? Add to this that some of Crane's friends distrusted his plan for *"The Bridge"* partly because they themselves disliked Walt Whitman and one has what Brom Weber calls the "death wish" that was "strong within him because of his inability to defend his belief." In the face of those whom Brom Weber describes as his "intellectual and artistic mentors," who "drove" Hart Crane into a corner, he tried to "delude himself . . . with desperate hope . . . into thinking that it was he who had faith in the future." Inevitably, since faith in the future was of the essence of his theme, the poem fell apart into fragments before it was finished. How could Hart Crane have completed *"The Bridge"* in the spirit in which he conceived it; and how, for that matter, could he have continued to live?

Now I have dwelt so long on the case of Rimbaud and Hart Crane only because it is emblematic of many other cases in which Americans, unsure of themselves, and unsure of their tradition, have literally followed strange gods to their own undoing. It is obvious that Hart Crane, in order to carry his great theme out, should have lived deeply in harmony with the *whole context* of his theme, should have turned a deaf ear to disbelievers in Whitman's ideas and gone his own way in defiance of the current fashion. And how many other American writers have been bewildered in a similar way by models who were essentially hostile to their own deepest aims. Half aware of a tradition of their own, as Hart Crane was, and prompted to write in the vein of this tradition, they were not aware of it sufficiently to withstand a fashion that opposed it in favor of totally different ideas. Too often, moreover, these ideas have had no connection with the writer's real nature or the social world he knows and in which he has been formed. How far did Crane, for instance, understand the peculiar conditions that produced the peculiar reaction of Rimbaud's ideas? —certainly no more than Sherwood Anderson understood D. H. Lawrence's world when he lost himself, in a measure, following Lawrence. When Anderson said, "I had a world and it slipped away from me," did he know that it *might not* have slipped if he had realized the nature of his gift as a folk storyteller and rejected every influence that was incongruous with it? Was he not, in his naïveté, spoiled in a way when, losing the thread of this gift, he began to see himself as the self-conscious artist, bedazzled by the circle of Gertrude Stein and what Thomas Wolfe called the "fancy" Americans, the "esthetic Americans" who became "more 'Flauberty' than Flaubert"? How often our writers seem to suggest the theme of Henry James, the betrayal of the "innocent" American by a "corrupt" old Europe, though the Europeans would be only too happy if Americans followed their natural bent instead of tagging blindly after them.

What this means is that American writers should not only know themselves but should know the deep world of feeling that lies behind them, a world that is really different from the European world and that has shaped the images which fill their minds. They should follow every influence that fortifies these, rejecting every influence that dissipates them, as they should know the laws of the literary life and see them in the light of their own tradition. Not that they should read too much or follow American models alone—how much Sherwood Anderson might have profited if he had studied Chekhov! And it would be impossible for teachers of literature to present too wide a range of models from the literature of the world. But is it not best, as one must have models, to have them on one's own terms, models, generally congruous with one's own conditions, who can illustrate the complex art of living as a writer and tell writers what they ought to know. These models can explain what Goethe meant when he said, "Spend not a moment's time with people to whom you do not belong and who do not belong to you," and they can show how far Virginia Woolf was right when she asked for "five hundred pounds a year and a room of one's own." They can show perhaps that the "life of pleasure" may be as "boring and painful" as it is to Aldous Huxley who has found rewarding the "narrow way of domestic duty" and "intellectual labor."

Well, then, if it has this value, is not our tradition worth exploring to find whatever models exist in the past—that is to say, if we are able to reach the past over the warscorched earth of the past few decades? For the world wars have disinherited innumerable sensitive American minds that have lost their sense alike of the past and the future, minds that have been conditioned, moreover, by their experience of war to a life that is not easily related to the life of our old writers. Even if there were no more wars it would take several decades for the agitated minds of the young writers of our day, accustomed to violence, excitement, and perpetual movement, to see that life as anything but tedious, insipid, flat, and dull. But how many good caretakers of their talents existed in that older world, in which the question of "frustration" was not omnipresent and in which there were at least a dozen writers regarding whom one could not say that they were "truncated" or "incomplete." What a wonderful example, for instance, was Hawthorne, with his four rules of life: to break off customs, to meditate on youth, to shake off spirits ill disposed and to do nothing against one's genius. Another was Thoreau, who said that a writer should saunter to his task surrounded by a halo of ease and leisure and who showed how far a man could arrange his life to make this possible by living without impedimenta on a few cents a day. What a quarry of practical wisdom for writers lies exposed, moreover, in some of Emerson's miscellaneous papers, suggestions of every sort, tonics for the torpid mind, stimulants and purgatives for minds that are untuned or crippled. One does not recollect this to shame the present with examples of the past or to magnify the importance of these writers; but is it not worth anyone's while to examine a period in one's own past that has had such substantial consequences? Not that writers should confine their explorations to a single American region—for one can find models now throughout the country, along with examples of the mistakes that writers fall into—in a day when the world is all before them, where to choose, and one may find models all over the planet. The important thing is that they should transcend the juvenile roles they so often perform—the role of the playboy, the tough guy, the groping adolescent—in which they perpetually repeat themselves and exploit their personalities until they are as tired of themselves as we are tired of them. Only the right models, rightly chosen to fit their special aptitudes, can jog them out of these roles into which they settle, models whom they are constrained to follow and who are a sort of superior selves, of the same nature with them but enlarged and ripened. Of what value are "moments of discovery" unless they lead to this?

XII

"SHOW ME THY GLORY"

BY

URSULA M. NIEBUHR

Then felt I like some watcher of the skies
When a new planet swims upon his ken.

The lines of Keats come to mind when we ponder the simple
words of the title given us, "A Moment of Discovery." Thus, perhaps,
we feel ourselves in the company of the scientist, or even of the alche-
mist of old, seeking the secret key to unlock the mystery of life. Shall
it be that we, too, at some specific point in time, are able to cry
"Eureka"—"I have discovered it"?

For some of us, however, it is not quite like this. The moment in the
search for meaning dawns upon us, even we might say, "discovers"
us, rather than we come upon, or discover it. Does not Keats make
us feel that it was as much he who was discovered by Chapman's
Homer, rather than the other way 'round?

Or like stout Cortez, when with eagle eyes,
He stared at the Pacific, and all his men
Looked at each other with a wild surmise
Silent upon a peak in Darien.

Those of us who accept the presuppositions of religious faith, would
agree, I am sure, that it is not so much that we discover new stages in
the unfolding of life's meaning, but that we are discovered by the
discovery.

So much as introduction to the very simple occasion which for me
brought light, and helped me to relate various aspects of thought and
interpretation. There is nothing to the story as such, but there *is*

point to a certain word which the occasion emphasized. Not only is it a word we find all through the Bible, but it is also a word which gives us a frame of reference against which we can put our concepts and our pictures of God and man.

Some years ago a Roman Catholic friend from abroad was spending the evening with us. We had been talking about many things; mutual friends, mutual interests, and theology. By the fire after dinner, we had spoken of the need as well as of the joy of having friends of congenial interests and thought, across the boundaries of nation, faith, or race. I had remarked, rather at large, and somewhat facetiously, that in some sense, and of course from one's own sinful perspective, the Church, the *ekklesia* or called-out ones, was bound to consist of oneself and one's friends. Our visitor replied, "Don't you suppose the Church *was* the Church when one or two could declare, '*We* beheld His glory'?"

I cannot remember what was said after that. Those few words, spoken so casually; and catching up other words, so well known and often studied, somehow bit into my consciousness. I had been working on the Fourth Gospel, using Sir Edwyn Hoshyn's great commentary which had just come out. As background for the Prologue I had been reading Exodus as according to the Septuagint, so I suppose my mind had been plowed, to a certain extent, and prepared for this sudden stimulus so casually given.

"We beheld His glory." Yes, that was the claim of the "called-out ones," the Church, Israel. Suddenly all the categories we use to describe what Religion is, in relation to life; what revelation is in relation to faith; who and what God is, in relation to the good—all these descriptions seemed inadequate and thin. The word, "glory, *Kabod*" or "*doxa*," with its association of light, splendor, and mystery suddenly made our conventional and customary descriptions and schemes of relationships seem as flat as rows or groups of labels. Instead, the word itself gave me the context, the framework in which to work.

The Bible speaks, in fact, I am tempted to say, *sings,* or *proclaims,* the glory of God. "The Heavens declare the glory of God," "Be thou exalted, O Lord, above the heavens; thy glory above the earth." As the heavens overarch the earth, so the glory of the Lord overarches and yet contains His mercy and His truth. The glory of God overwhelms, and yet leads His people; it is displayed to Moses, and to other holy men and prophets, and is described as eternal and yet historically relevant, and is envoked both as memory and as hope. "Glory to God in the Highest."

We can investigate the word, and notice the various emphases and interpretations, in Hebrew, in Greek, and even in English. Here must be mentioned the three well known but sadly still out of print lectures by the late Israel Abrahams, given in New York in 1924, at the Jewish Institute of Religion and the Hebrew Union College in Cincinnati, as well as the excellent study by then Professor and now Bishop Arthur Michael Ramsey, "The Glory of God and the Transfiguration of Christ." [1] But without going into the exact study of the word with its fascinating history, let us ask the question, how many others also have suddenly waked to its pull and attraction? Does it not catch us up to a realm of images and concepts suggested by story after story in the Bible? We recall Moses before the Burning Bush; Moses on the Mount; Isaiah in the Temple, seeing the Lord high and lifted up; Ezekiel before the appearance of the likeness of the Glory of the Lord; the Transfiguration of Jesus on the Mount; St. Paul on the way to Damascus; the vision of the New Jerusalem in the Apocalypse of St. John the Divine. Even in our use of the English words, "glory" or "glorious," we express a little of the over and above-ness of the ordinary which needs God to fulfil it. It is in English one of the few words that has not been debased even by our common coin of speech. In casual use, glory is suggested by the rays of the sun, by the halos round the heads of saints and holy persons; by the honor and praise we give the extraordinary which judges our ordinary. "What a glorious day," we say, or, "such-and-such an experience was too glorious for words." Glory is more than beauty, more than mystery as such, more than goodness. The Hebrew word and conceptions which lie behind the Greek word of the New Testament stand for

[1] Israel Abrahams, *The Glory of God*, Oxford University Press, London, 1925.

A. M. Ramsey, *The Glory of God and the Transfiguration of Christ*, Longmans, Green & Company, Ltd., London, 1949.

the qualities and appurtenances of God, and suggest as well as describe His Presence, which is too glorious for man to behold. Yet also, His glory is "shed abroad," shines forth; visits men; and in the New Testament, is tabernacled with men. Man, the creature and the child of God, is bidden to offer praise and glory back to God, so that God and His creatures are linked together, as Charles Williams has remarked, by the very filaments of his Glory.

But this word of splendor does more than enchant us with its wealth of association. It gives an exact description of God's nature in action. The glory of God is made explicit in His mercy and His truth, and the pattern of the glory of God was and is the pattern shown forth in His mighty works of mercy, or love, and truth or faithfulness. "We beheld His glory, glory as of the only-begotten of the Father, full of grace and truth." This was the witness of faith to the character and quality of the life, teaching, and death of Jesus. To the early Christian disciples, that life, teaching, and death were "full of grace and truth" indeed, but full, superabundantly: for the glory of God is the context of His mighty acts, a context we can accept or behold but cannot penetrate. Nor can we reproduce the glory, but we do seek to imitate and to reciprocate the mercy and the truth.

Perhaps then, glory becomes relevant as a word and as a concept, in three ways. First, glory describes the context of our call. We stand with Moses, with Isaiah, with Ezekiel. It may be that we do not always understand the glory, and, as St. Peter at the Transfiguration perhaps we "wist not what to say." But also, in spite of not understanding, we can say with Jacob, "Surely the Lord is in this place."

Then, secondly, glory is the context of the reference when we test our decisions and our understanding of our vocation. We want to be sure, dead sure, that the promises of God implied in His call and promises, are faithful and true. We recall the story of Moses arguing with God, in Exodus, 33.

And Moses said unto the Lord: "See, thou sayest unto me, 'Bring up this people': but thou hast not let me know whom thou wilt send with me. Yet thou hast said, 'I know you by name, and you have also found favour in my sight.' Now therefore, I pray thee, if I have found favour in thy sight, show me now thy ways, that I may know thee and find favour in thy sight. Consider too that this nation is thy people."

And he said, "My presence will go with thee, and I will give you rest."

And he said to him, "If thy presence will not go with me, do not carry us up from here. For how shall it be known that I have found favour in thy sight, I and thy people? Is it not in thy going with us, so that we are distinct, I and thy people, from all other people that are upon the face of the earth?"

And the Lord said to Moses, "This very thing that you have spoken, I will do; for you have found favour in my sight, and I know you by name."

Moses said, "I pray thee, show me thy glory."

And he said, "I will make all my goodness pass before you, and will proclaim before you my name, 'The Lord,' and I will be gracious to whom I will be gracious, and will show mercy to whom I will show mercy. But," he said, "you cannot see my face; for man shall not see me and live."

And the Lord said, "Behold, there is a place by me where you shall stand upon the rock; and while my glory passes by I will put you in a cleft of the rock, and I will cover you with my hand until I have passed by; then I will take away my hand, and you shall see my back; but my face shall not be seen."

This is the story of Moses, but it is also our story. Do not we ask for God's approval on our calling; on our commitments? Do not we pray that our actions and enterprises be accepted as right and good for us and for others? Moses asked for the assurance of God's favor and approval for himself, for his calling, and for his people. "Show me now thy ways, that I may know thee, that I may find favour in thy sight. Consider too that this nation is thy people." It should be noticed that he did not ask for benefits, for signs of God's approval. Instead, he asked that God might show him "His ways"; and that he, Moses, might know God.

His prayer was that his calling might be found to be authentic, to be valid, yet the climax of his intercession is not in the request for the certifying of himself or his cause, but comes in the simple petition: "Show me, I pray thee, thy glory." As ever in the Bible, the glory, which is the presence, the mystery, and the power of God, is the context against which man's search for meaning is placed. Thus, the showing of the glory is followed in this story of the Yahwehistic source in Exodus by the proclamation of God's will, His "ways" for His people, in the form of the Law written on the tablets of stone. For Israel thereafter the Law was the expression of God's truth or faithfulness and mercy. All through the Old Testament, the holy and humble men of heart turn back to that occasion "He made known His ways to Moses" (Psalm 103.7) and echo the very words of Moses: "Make me to know thy ways, O Lord; teach me thy paths. Lead me in thy truth and teach me" (Psalm 25.4, 5). The righteous man, the man of integrity and truth is he that "walketh in the way of the Lord": "Vindicate me, O Lord, for I have walked in my integrity, for thy steadfast love is before my eyes, and I walk in faithfulness to thee" (Psalm 26.1, 3).

But the story of Israel's vocation in the Old Testament is the story of the truth and mercy of God as understood or as misunderstood by Israel. God's justice as the expression of His truth in history, His love as the expression of His mercy, the tension between these for Israel—as for us today—was constant. The great questions and deep searchings of Jeremiah and Job place God's truth and justice above human reckoning. Deutero-Isaiah, echoing Hosea and Jeremiah, but going so much further, not only describes the vocation of God's servant in terms of suffering love, but also shows the steadfastness and strange self-consistency of such love.

We stand with Moses. We follow the story of faith in the Old Testament, and tread in the steps of those who sought for the meaning of truth and mercy in the nature of God as described in His Law, and revealed through His prophets. The story starts with Moses, "Show me, I pray thee, thy glory." For some of us, this prayer looks to the Word made Flesh and tabernacled with men, and the witness of Christian faith is that "we beheld His glory, . . . full of grace and truth." But all of us, Jew and Christian alike, stand in hope of glory. All of us ascribe to God the Kingdom, power and *glory*. And it is this attitude of hope which surely is the third way the word, "glory," is related to our thinking and our living. It is by hope that we declare that we are children of God and heirs of His Kingdom. Hope is so often identified with optimism either about ourselves or about immediate possibilities that hope in the context of the glory of God is not understood. "Thine is the Kingdom, the power *and* the glory." What a magnificent declaration of faith and hope. The *real,* the final glory is God's and God's alone. All our proximate hopes and efforts are offered as we echo the words. For how dare we ascribe glory to ourselves or anything else under heaven when we think of the glory of God? Yet all of God's world has value through its relation to Him and His plan of salvation. So we offer to God His own works which so often reflect His glory; deeds of love and valor, the beauty of art and music, the order and the meaning of literature and science, for, indeed as St. Paul said (Romans 8.28), "We know that in everything God works together for good with those who love Him, who are called according to His purpose."

The "hope of glory," then, holds us in a "glorious" fellowship. Here, perhaps, may be allowed a protest against those who make of religion, of religious teaching, or of worship, a *dull* thing. Dullness should be classified as heresy. It is really a contradiction of religion. In the Bible, religion is the story of the relation of God and man, Heaven and earth, and that story is set in the framework of glory. Can glory, real glory, be dull? Our traditional forms of worship, Jewish and Christian, echo the same theme of glory. When we look for creation itself to obtain the glorious freedom of the children of God, there is one thing which can be quite confidently stated. In the realm of glory not only "death shall be no more," neither "mourning nor crying nor pain," but also neither shall there be *dullness* any more.

CONTRIBUTORS TO "THE HOUR OF INSIGHT" *

VAN WYCK BROOKS, A.B., Litt.D., Columbia University, Dartmouth University, etc.; Fellow, Conference on Science, Philosophy and Religion; Author: *The Times of Melville and Whitman, A Chilmark Miscellany, The Confident Years,* and others.

IRVING BEN COOPER, LL.B., Washington University; Chief Justice, Court of Special Sessions, New York City.

KARL W. DEUTSCH, Ph.D., Harvard University, Dr. Pol.Sci., Charles University, Prague; Professor of History and Political Science, Massachusetts Institute of Technology; Fellow, Conference on Science, Philosophy and Religion.

HOXIE N. FAIRCHILD, Ph.D., Columbia University; Professor of English, Hunter College of the City of New York; Fellow, Conference on Science, Philosophy and Religion; Author: *The Romantic Quest, Toward Belief, Religious Trends in English Poetry,* and others.

JOHN FERREN, Painter; Instructor of Painting, The Cooper Union; Lecturer in Art, Queens College.

SIMON GREENBERG, Ph.D., Dropsie College, Rabbi, The Jewish Theological Seminary of America; Vice-Chancellor and Professor of Homiletics, The Jewish Theological Seminary of America; Member, Board of Directors, Conference on Science, Philosophy and Religion; Member, Executive Committee, The Institute for Religious and Social Studies; Author: *Ideas and Ideals in the Jewish Prayer Book, The First Year in the Hebrew School: A Teacher's Guide,* and others.

HUDSON HOAGLAND, Ph.D., Harvard University; Executive Director, The Worcester Foundation for Experimental Biology; Fellow, Conference on Science, Philosophy and Religion; Author: *Pacemakers in Relation to Aspects of Behavior;* Co-editor: *Experimental Biology Monographs.*

STEPHEN S. KAYSER, Ph.D., Heidelberg University; Curator, The Jewish Museum, The Jewish Theological Seminary of America.

* As of February, 1953.

137

INDEX

Abrahams, Israel, 131
ACTH, 11, 12
Activation energy, 4, 5
Adams, Henry, 116
Adrenal cortex:
  cortisone from, 11
  fatigue and, 10-11
  schizophrenic patients and, 12
AE, on writers, 122
Africa, tuberculosis in, 38-39
Ambition, 101-102
American Indians, tuberculosis among, 38
American literature:
  concentration on form, 118
  literature of boys, 115
  tradition and, 125
  youth cult of writers, 115-116, 118
Anderson, Sherwood, 115, 116, 125, 126
Anthropology, 15-28
antiSemitism, 103
  in Southern Germany, 42
Anxiety, and disease, 36
Arofa, of Tikopia, 24-25
Arrhenius equation, 3-6
Art:
  abstract movement in, 55
  Jewish ritual, 49
Artificial fevers, 4
  time sense and, 5
Artificial insemination, 8
Artist:
  and nature, 53
  true function of, 54
Assimilation, problems of, 81-82
Auden, W. H., 79
Auerbach, Berthold, 42, 43
Austria, remembrances of, 74-75

Baden, Grand Duchy of, 42
Baptism, 85
Baudelaire, Pierre Charles, 122, 123

Behavior:
  cycles, rhythms of, 2-3
  disease and, 29-39
  family patterns of, 34
Berlin Movement, 43
Besant, Annie, 58
Biochemistry, 2
Birth control, among Tikopia, 28
Blood pressure, 36
Bois, Jules, 118-119
Boll, Franz, 46
Brand names and preferences, 81
Braque, Georges, 55, 57
Bridge, The (Hart Crane), 124, 125
Brooks, Van Wyck:
  early reading of, 113-115
  paper by, 113-127
  sketch of, 137
Buber, Martin, 45
Bush, Wendell, 1

Cancer, sex hormones and, 9
Catholicism, 79
Central Europe, leader in, 76-77
Change:
  and disease, 37-39
  chemical, 3-4
Chemical change, 3-4
Childrearing among Tikopia, 17-20
Christianity, and social service, 69
Cicero, 122
Clark University, 9, 10
Coldblooded animals, 6
Colitis, ulcerative, 33, 35
Communism of 1930's, 78
Confession, 51
Cooper, Irving Ben:
  admitted to Bar, 62
  childhood of, 61
  early reading of, 61-62
  first case, 63-64